Published by
National Railway Museum
York
1992

ISBN No. 1 872826 01 6

Printed by Ian Allan Printing Ltd, Coombelands House, Addlestone, Surrey KT15 1HY

Perspectives on
RAILWAY HISTORY
and interpretation

Essays to celebrate the work of
Dr John Coiley
at the National Railway Museum, York

Edited by

Neil Cossons   **Allan Patmore**   **Rob Shorland–Ball**

National Railway Museum York

Contents

Page

THE NATIONAL RAILWAY COLLECTION

MUSEUM INTERPRETATION

Dr John Coiley, Keeper of the
National Railway Museum, York
1975 – 1992

Editors' Foreword

In his seventeen years in charge of the National Railway Museum, John Coiley inspired great affection and respect amongst colleagues and friends. Both affection and respect had many roots, but none more profound than the universal admiration of his encyclopaedic knowledge and scholarship on the whole subject of railways. In seeking to mark his retirement in a very special way, the idea naturally arose of a volume of essays dedicated to him, with contributions from among his colleagues and friends.

This, then, is the genesis of this book. Its themes are as varied as the interests of its authors. They do, however, fall into three distinct groups and these need a brief initial comment. The largest group, the first seven essays, are all original studies of some aspect of railway history or the wider impact of railways. The following five essays are concerned with the NRM, and its precursors, as repositories of railway material. Several of these essays concern material which is a part of the NRM collections but not necessarily on public display and give a glimpse of the depth of knowledge about the collections which is so much a part of the NRM tradition. The final group of essays looks at the wider issues of displaying and interpreting the collections. They range from an early critique of the NRM to a record of the changes between 1988 and 1992 which have developed the scope of the Museum almost beyond recognition.

In preparing this collection of essays for printing, the editors are deeply grateful to a large number of people. First and foremost are the contributors, who produced manuscripts to very tight deadlines and gave their enthusiasm and talents without stint. In production, many skills in the Museum were used, but particular mention must be made of Liz Culyer who retyped a very miscellaneous clutch of manuscripts with speed, precision and elegance, and of Glenn Atkinson whose design skills in desktop publishing translated typescript to book format ready for the printer. In the Museum office Philippa Woolven and Angela Chatterton were invaluable in sorting, photocopying and dealing with the huge post generated by the request for subscriptions with patience and efficiency. Finally, we would mention our subscribers, whose financial contribution made the whole venture possible, and whose faith thus displayed was the best of all tributes to the regard in which John Coiley – and 'his' Museum – are held.

Neil Cossons *Allan Patmore* *Rob Shorland–Ball*

Introduction

Neil Cossons

'One thing is done supremely well at York. This museum alone can lead the visitor back continuously, stage by stage, over the whole history of railways in Britain – beyond the passenger–carrying train and the steam locomotive to the colliery lines and the wooden waggonways of Northumberland and Durham, out of which, in the eighteenth century, the modern railway began to emerge'.[1]

With these words Professor Jack Simmons concluded his description of the Railway Museum, York. The museum to which he was referring was not the National Railway Museum, but its predecessor, a museum whose origins lay in the sense of history and tradition felt so strongly in the North East of England and which the Railways Act of 1921 and the creation of the 'Big Four' companies appeared to threaten. The North Eastern Railway, with its headquarters in York, embraced the whole of this territory of early railway development, and it had incorporated the Stockton & Darlington Railway – the oldest steam powered public railway in the world. It thus held, in every sense, the inheritance of George and Robert Stephenson and their predecessors. Its independent existence about to end with the formation of the London & North Eastern Railway, attention turned to preserving something of its origins. Efforts were led by a Railway Museum Committee, chaired by J B Harper, Assistant Superintendent at York, and the result was a collection housed initially in the basement of the North Eastern offices in the city. Like other collections of its type – there was another at Paddington – it remained private, but as a result of the centenary celebrations of the Stockton & Darlington in 1925, pressure mounted for a public museum and this opened in the old locomotive erecting and repair shop of the York & North Midland Railway in 1928. The rest of this story, and the subsequent events leading to the creation of the National Railway Museum and its opening in September 1975, are set out elsewhere in this book.

York's historical credentials to be the home of the National Railway Museum are impeccable and the geographical and cultural benefits resulting from the placing of a major national museum outside London have been proved beyond all doubt. It is important too that it is one of the group of museums that form the National Museum of Science & Industry, the others being the Science Museum, London, and the National Museum of Photography, Film & Television in Bradford. This makes York part of an even longer tradition of railway preservation going back to the years after the Great Exhibition of 1851. *Puffing Billy*, *Rocket* and *Sans Pareil*, currently on display in the Science Museum, are the most visible reminders of these earliest efforts to ensure that the origins of the steam railway were immortalised in an appropriate manner.

Today the National Railway Collection forms an incomparable resource, not only for the study of the railway but as a means of conveying to a wider audience a sense of the immense impact the railway has had on the lives of all of us. Since the National Railway Museum opened in 1975 the collections have continued to grow on all fronts. The Museum's library, archive and photographic holdings have all developed steadily under the guidance of expert and enthusiastic staff. Locomotives and rolling stock, made available through the special relationship with British Rail, have been carefully selected to reflect as accurately as possible change and development in contemporary railway practice. Completeness is impossible – and neither necessary nor desirable. The work of the curator is to maintain a balance between the inevitable desire for comprehensiveness and the practical and financial consequences of achieving that. This is particularly critical with large railway material, where although the costs of acquisition are usually minimal, the long term commitment to conservation – preventative and remedial – represents a continuing and growing responsibility.

And it is the collections which form the lifeblood of the Museum. Our prime responsibility is to build those collections and care for them in perpetuity. They are not an exploitable asset to be used and thrown away, nor to be traded, but an integral part of the nation's culture, to be protected and passed on to future generations. It is salutary to remind ourselves that there are objects in our care that have been part of the National Railway Collection for over one hundred and thirty years. That fact alone defines the guiding principle by which the Museum's work must be conducted.

This process of building collections and providing proper care for them has been managed supremely well at York. The Museum has risen to the daunting task set for it – of being both the repository for the material evidence of the railway and a centre where that evidence, in the form of the National Railway Collection, can inspire and educate the visitor. Those visitors, as we know from our audience research, are less familiar with the railway than their predecessors were seventeen years ago when the Museum opened. The generations for whom the steam railway was a central part of their lives are passing. The nature and the role of the railway is changing too. A renaissance is under way. The railway is now the subject of massive capital development in all leading European countries. The new continental network of railways, of which Britain becomes a part with the opening of the Channel Tunnel, will lead to a new railway age. It will be the job of the National Railway Museum to reflect those developments and place them in the context of the long history of the railway.

Throughout the period from before its opening and up to the eve of its new period of growth and development, the National Railway Museum was presided over by John Coiley. John joined the Science Museum in 1973 from industry. His background was in metallurgy and his career to that date had largely been concerned with research. But he brought with him a life–long interest in and knowledge of railways and he arrived in the Museum as the final stages of the York initiative were taking shape. In 1974 he was appointed Keeper and he saw the Museum through to its successful opening by HRH the Duke of Edinburgh on 27 September 1975, the one hundred and fiftieth anniversary of the opening of the Stockton & Darlington Railway.

The Museum was an immediate and outstanding success. Over one million visitors attended in its first year. Indeed the setting up of the National Railway Museum in York, the first move by a London national museum to establish a major collection outside the capital, set the pattern which others have followed.

Throughout the seventies and eighties the collections continued to grow, paralleled by a programme of conservation and restoration. Additional accommodation was acquired, notably the Railway Goods Depot across Leeman Road from the main Museum. By the mid–1980s plans were being formulated to open the depot (now named the Peter Allen Building after the Museum Advisory Committee's past Chairman, Sir Peter Allen), thereby almost doubling the size of the Museum, when serious structural problems were encountered with the roof of the original hall. A major programme to replace the roof, which included the transfer of the collections to two temporary exhibitions – one in York and the other in Swindon – meant that the core of the National Railway Collection was maintained on view to the public throughout. The exhibition in York – The Great Railway Show – won the Museum of the Year Award for the National Railway Museum in 1991. With the completion of the roof the locomotives and rolling stock were returned to York and plans for expanding the Museum continued, leading to the opening in April 1992.

John Coiley retired in January 1992, on the eve of the last stage of the programme of renewal and expansion. During his seventeen years in charge of the Museum its stature and authority in the field of railway history and preservation matured. Today the National Railway Museum stands as a shining example of responsible acquisition and conservation, as a prime source for the railway historian and as a place where the general public may gain an insight into the origins and subsequent development of that most remarkable phenomenon of the nineteenth century – the railway.

This volume salutes John Coiley's part in that process. It has been put together by his friends and colleagues[2] as a tribute to his leadership of the National Railway Museum and as a measure of our respect for all he has contributed in bringing the railway to the public.

Science Museum
March 1992

Notes and References

1. J. Simmons, *Transport Museums* George Allen and Unwin, 1970. p158
2. I am particularly grateful to Professor Allan Patmore and Rob Shorland-Ball for their editorial work.

1 The railway drawings of John Wilson Carmichael

Richard Durack

John Wilson Carmichael was one of many artists to turn his attention towards the railway during the first half of the nineteenth century. This was a period when railways were still a novelty and it is difficult today to understand the excitement that was created by this new form of transport. The first steam locomotives to appear quickly caught the attention of the public. Interest increased with the opening of the Stockton & Darlington Railway but it was the Liverpool & Manchester Railway that first received widespread notice. Its opening in 1830 caused a national sensation and enormous amounts of memorabilia, including prints and illustrations, were produced. It has been estimated that no fewer than two thousand prints of railway subjects were published during the period from 1830 to 1850 and scarcely a line opened without at least one view being issued. Publishers commissioned work from a wide range of artists to satisfy this demand and were helped by advances in printing technology. The development of engraving on steel plates, rather than the softer copper, enabled detailed work to be printed more easily and most artists including Carmichael began to have their work engraved on steel. Carmichael is best known for his series of views of the Newcastle & Carlisle Railway but these are only part of his output on railway and engineering subjects. He went on to produce several studies of bridges and viaducts in his native north–east as well as two oil paintings of similar structures in Sussex. His work is well represented in the collections at the National Railway Museum.

Carmichael was born in 1799 in Newcastle upon Tyne. He went to sea at an early age and on his return was apprenticed as a shipwright to a Newcastle firm of shipbuilders. It was here that his artistic talents became apparent and seem to have been encouraged. As an artist he was largely self–taught although he was given some training in draughtsmanship and may also have received tuition from Thomas Miles Richardson, the well–known Newcastle landscape painter. By 1823 he had become a full–time artist producing both landscape and marine views. It was as a painter of seascapes, sea battles and river life that he was to achieve his greatest fame but he could turn his hand to a variety of subjects. His industrial and railway studies, although important for the railway historian, never formed a major part of his output but he did continue with his landscape work. He enjoyed a long and close working relationship with John Dobson, the Newcastle architect, and added colour and detail to many of Dobson's drawings including two fine views of the interior and exterior of the new Central Station in Newcastle designed by Dobson and opened in 1850.[1] Carmichael was a relentless worker and often completed a painting a day. He was described by William Bell Scott, who had arrived in Newcastle in 1840 to run the Government School of Design, as "...bluff and generous, and a friendlier and more honourable man it would have been difficult to find......a good specimen of the ready, energetic, indefatigable Northumbrian".[2]

In 1846 Carmichael moved to London where he continued his marine work and accepted other commissions. In 1855 he was employed by the *Illustrated London News* to sketch scenes in the Baltic campaign of the Crimean War. He died in Scarborough in 1868.

Carmichael produced a series of twenty–four drawings of the Newcastle & Carlisle Railway which were published by Currie and Bowman of Newcastle upon Tyne. The first four were issued in 1836 followed by four more the following year and the final sixteen in 1838. In 1839 all twenty–four were published together under the title *Views on the Newcastle and Carlisle Railway* which contained an accompanying text by John Blackmore, Engineer to the Company, describing each view.[3]

Plate 1.1
The Depot at Hexham. *1836*

The Newcastle & Carlisle was an important line and the first route to be built across Britain. Work had begun in 1830 and the first section, between Blaydon and Hexham, was opened in 1835. The main section at the western end, between Carlisle and Greenhead, was completed in the following year but it was not until June 1838 that the gap between the two sections was closed. Even then passengers could only reach Newcastle by travelling along the Redheugh branch of the line and crossing the Tyne by ferry. It was only in the following year that the line along the north bank of the river, via the new bridge at Scotswood, was opened and passengers were able to reach the new terminus at the Shot Tower on the western edge of the City.

Construction had not presented major problems. At the eastern end delays had been caused by the periodic flooding of the Tyne but it was in the west that most difficulties were encountered. The line had originally been planned to follow the River Irthing, which would have provided a gradual descent into Carlisle, but this was abandoned in favour of a route to the south which required more extensive engineering work. Viaducts were built across the rivers Eden and Gelt, as well as the Corby Burn, and construction also involved the creation of a major embankment at Hell Beck and a cutting over a mile in length through the Cowran Hills. It had originally been intended to build a tunnel at this point but loose sand and gushing springs had made this impossible. The Newcastle & Carlisle was not a line built for speed. "Whoever is in the habit of travelling on the railway between Newcastle and Carlisle will be forcibly struck with the sinuosities of its course throughout..." wrote Francis Whishaw in *The Railways of Great Britain and Ireland* in 1840 "...A snakelike motion, and frequent jerks, are consequences of this curvilinear course; and unless it had been originally laid out for a railway or tram–road to be worked by horses, no engineer would have ventured to recommend a plan which exhibits on the face of it almost one continuous series of curves from end to end".[4]

Whishaw is clearly guilty of exaggeration but Carmichael reveals few straight stretches of track as he shows the line following the contours of the landscape in a series of neat and ordered views. All the most important engineering structures are included and the scenes of activity on the Tyne looking towards Newcastle and in the depot yard at Hexham give an impression of exciting enterprise. Industry, an important source of revenue, is not neglected either and both Wylam Colliery and the lime kilns at Allerwash are featured. But above all Carmichael shows a line winding its way through a picturesque landscape where the railway is almost of secondary interest. Cows continue to graze undisturbed and fishermen and the local hunt go about their business as trains pass by. Groups of peasants or the admiring gentry stand idly at the side of the line or sit on horseback. The views are timeless and the railway could have been part of the scenery for a hundred years so well does it blend into the background.

Plate 1.2
Allerwash. *1838*

3

Plate 1.3
The River Wall at Wylam Scars.
1836

The work of Carmichael and other artists did much to dispel the fear and dislike of this new form of transport. Many were afraid of the dangers of explosions or accidents while others predicted that passengers would suffocate in tunnels or find it impossible to breathe when travelling at speed. Hostility was widespread to the noise and smoke of the locomotives and to the disruption that the railway caused. Railway promoters and directors welcomed prints and illustrations as a way of overcoming prejudice and publishers were often sympathetic to the railway cause. *Views on the Newcastle and Carlisle Railway* was not only dedicated to the Chairman and Directors of the Company "...to whom the proprietors and the public are much indebted for their zeal and perseverance in forwarding that great national and local object..." but was also "...undertaken at their suggestion".[5] The Newcastle & Carlisle had faced its share of opposition and its greatest antagonist had been Charles Bacon of Styford Hall near Riding Mill. Bacon had tried to stop the construction of the line and he also objected after it opened when the Company began to use locomotives in contravention of its Act of Parliament. Trains were halted for over a month before he was persuaded to withdraw his opposition. Landowners were generally in favour of railway development provided that they received adequate compensation and the line passed a respectable distance from their house. Many were involved as promoters or investors and recognised the economic benefits that the railway would bring. Two of the strongest supporters of the Newcastle & Carlisle were Thomas Wentworth Beaumont of Bywell Hall and Colonel J B Coulson of Blenkinsopp Hall. Carmichael included both houses in his series of views.

Carmichael based his finished engravings on a series of on–the–spot sketches that he carried out along the line between 1835 and 1837. These have survived and are now held in the collections of Carlisle Museum and Art Gallery and the Laing Art Gallery in Newcastle upon Tyne. They take the form of pencil drawings to which watercolour was sometimes added as well as notes on colour and detail. Although they are less polished than the finished views they are generally a more valuable source of information for the railway historian. Several formed the basis for finished engravings and show the way in which Carmichael worked and how he would build up a composition. The sketch would first be altered slightly to create greater dramatic effect. Angles were often made sharper so that engineering structures would appear more impressive while trees and buildings would be moved and light and shade varied to produce a more unified design. Detail would then be added. Few of the sketches contain figures and Carmichael would add these, especially in the foreground, to draw the eye into the picture in exactly the same way as he did with his marine work. He made many drawings from life throughout his career and was able to draw on the contents of his sketchbooks to flesh out and fill in the detail of any composition.

Carmichael treated locomotives and trains in much the same way as figures. They occasionally appear in the sketches but only in rough outline. Sometimes they are the opposite way round to the finished engraving as in the sketch of Prudhoe Castle and Ovingham.[6] Elsewhere there is often a note of where they are to go. "Put the trains at this end" has been added to the sketch of the River–Wall at Wylam Scars[7] while the sketch of the Depot at Hexham contains the instruction "engine first, then some low waggons full of casks, boxes, lead, hay, etc. Then comes the passengers".[8] This use of locomotives and rolling stock as a compositional device does raise the question of accuracy. There are great dangers in accepting the technical detail in railway engravings as historical evidence but there is good reason to believe that the work of Carmichael is more reliable than most. His training in draughtsmanship and the reputation for accuracy that he acquired for his shipping studies suggest that he would have taken equal care with other subjects. Drawings of railway equipment appear in his sketchbooks and he is known to have made at least one study of a locomotive on the line.[9] Where he does come unstuck is in showing trains travelling on the wrong tracks. The Newcastle & Carlisle was one of the few railways in Britain where trains ran on the right–hand side in double–track sections. In two of his engravings Carmichael shows them travelling on the left.

Most of the sketches that Carmichael produced were not used for the finished views but are still of great interest. This is particularly the case with the eighteen sketches held at Carlisle Museum and Art Gallery. All were completed during 1835, the earliest period that Carmichael is known to have worked on the project, and they not only show the line still under construction but also provide evidence that is not available in the finished engravings. The two studies of Carlisle that were published were particularly disappointing in comparison with the five sketches that Carmichael drew of the City. Three of these show work in progress on the Canal Branch of the line which was opened from London Road, the main terminus in Carlisle, to the Canal Basin in 1837. The line ran to the south and west of Carlisle and one sketch shows work in progress on the bridge that was constructed over the River Caldew.[10] Two further sketches feature the Canal Basin itself with its warehouses and ships. The new train shed and other railway buildings are also shown together with a breakdown crane and other items of railway equipment.[11]

Construction work is shown on other sections of the line too. At Scotby Embankment stone blocks are being cut and laid to take the rails.[12] Two sketches feature work in progress on the cutting through the Cowran Hills. Much of the soil that was excavated was used to build the embankment further to the west but a great deal still had to be removed. Carmichael shows spoil trucks on the floor of the cutting as well as the hoist that lifted trucks out of the cutting so that the spoil could be dumped.[13] There are also four sketches of the Gelt Bridge and two of these show building work in progress. Scaffolding supports the arches while men work on the stonework from a platform which has been lowered from the parapet to run across the width of the bridge. A hoist is being used to bring materials up to the deck of the bridge from the yards and workshops on the valley floor.[14] This collection of working sketches is unlike any of the finished engravings and invites comparison with the work of John Cooke Bourne who produced a similar series of drawings showing the construction of the London & Birmingham Railway.

In addition to the pencil sketches that it holds the Laing Art Gallery also has a number of small sepia drawings by Carmichael that he prepared for the engravers to work from. Several of the early railway artists, including Bourne and Arthur Fitzwilliam Tait, engraved their own views but Carmichael was happy to leave it to others. No fewer than nine engravers were employed to produce the series on the Newcastle & Carlisle Railway including Thomas Prior, best known for his engraving of the work of Turner, and Thomas Hair, a landscape painter who produced an impressive collection of sketches of the coal mines of Northumberland and Durham. It was rare for an engraver to make changes to a prepared drawing but this does seem to have happened to the view of the Arch under the Military Road near Naworth Castle which was used as the frontispiece to *Views on the Newcastle and Carlisle Railway*. Carmichael based his drawing on a pencil sketch that showed the completed bridge but little more.[15] Detail was then added and included two figures standing at the foot of the bridge in the path of an oncoming train.[16] Both had disappeared by the time the engraving was published and had been replaced by a shovel propped against the wall. Safety was a sensitive subject in these early years and many people were deceived by the speed of the new locomotives. Accidents were far from uncommon although the Newcastle & Carlisle had a better safety record than most other lines.

Plate 1.4
Arch under Military Road near
Naworth Castle (frontispiece).
1836

Plate 1.5
Victoria Bridge over the River
Wear. *1838*

Carmichael had a further three views of railway subjects published during 1838 while he was still working on his Newcastle & Carlisle series. The first was again issued by Currie and Bowman and featured the Victoria Bridge over the River Wear on the Durham Junction Railway. The other two were of the Willington Dene Viaduct and Ouseburn Viaduct on the Newcastle & North Shields Railway. Both were commissioned by Mark Lambert of Newcastle upon Tyne who had published a series of engravings by Carmichael several years earlier under the title *Views of the Tyne*. Copies of all three views are held by the National Railway Museum[17] as well as a small watercolour of the Ouseburn Viaduct which may have been produced for the engraver to work from.[18] Carmichael composed very similar views of these newly–completed structures and managed to include river scenes in the foreground of two of them. Thomas Miles Richardson also produced studies of the Willington Dene and Ouseburn Viaducts and provides more detail than Carmichael of their unorthodox construction. Both were built entirely of laminated timber arches resting on masonry piers, similar to the Wiebeking system used in the Pont d'Ivry in Paris. The architects, John and Benjamin Green, used the same method of construction for the roof of North Shields Station and a further bridge in Borough Road, North Shields. A section of this bridge is now held in the collections at the National Railway Museum.[19] The timber in both the Willington Dene and Ouseburn Viaducts was replaced later in the nineteenth century with iron although their appearance remained largely unaltered.

Plate 1.6
Willington Dene Viaduct. *1838*

All three of these views were engraved by George Hawkins who produced many fine studies of railway subjects, as both artist and engraver, including a series featuring the construction of the Britannia and Conway Tubular Bridges. It was also Hawkins who engraved the spectacular view of the projected High Level Bridge across the Tyne which Carmichael completed in 1846.[20] This was based on an oil painting which had been commissioned from Carmichael by the Directors of the York, Newcastle & Berwick Railway Company and is now held by the University of Newcastle upon Tyne. It involved Carmichael in a feat of great artistic imagination as construction work had yet to begin. He copied the plans of the new bridge and skillfully incorporated them into the existing landscape which included the Tyne Bridge and several notable buildings on the Newcastle side of the river. A little selective demolition work was also required as the *Gateshead Observer* reported:

> "....the primary object being a picture of the two bridges, and there being no vacant site commanding a good view of the two structures, the artist has taken the liberty to pull down (in imagination) the house at the south–eastern corner of Tyne Bridge and thus accomplish his design".[21]

Plate 1.7
Ouseburn Viaduct. Watercolour.
1838

Plate 1.8
Projected High Level Bridge at
Newcastle upon Tyne. *1846*

After his move to London Carmichael concentrated increasingly on shipping
subjects although in 1848 he exhibited two paintings at the Royal Academy of
viaducts on the London Brighton & South Coast Railway. One of these was of
the London Road Viaduct in Brighton which had been completed two years
earlier when the branch to Lewes was opened. This painting was lost for many
years but in 1955 it reappeared in an antique shop in York and was offered to
John Scholes, Curator of Relics with the former British Transport Commission.
There was some difficulty at first in identifying the location. "I have now
ascertained that there were *no* windmills in Scotland..." wrote Scholes in
September 1955[22] and he then wrote to several of the Regional Civil Engineers of
British Railways who soon came to his rescue. The painting was purchased by the
National Art Collections Fund and presented to the Commission for display at
the Railway Museum in York. It was transferred to the National Railway
Museum in 1975.[23] Carmichael painted his view from the north–west at a time
when the viaduct was still on the outskirts of Brighton. The scene is very different
today as the town has grown and houses have been built under the arches. The
viaduct was badly damaged by a bomb in 1943 and the temporary repair was the
subject of a painting by Sir Muirhead Bone. This painting, which shows two
locomotives being used for deflection tests on the temporary span, was displayed
in the Southern Railway boardroom at Waterloo for many years and is now held
by Brighton Art Gallery.

Carmichael may not have been the most exciting or innovative of the early railway
artists but the importance of his work should not be underestimated. Pictorial
evidence can never be wholly trusted but it is clear that he went to more trouble
than many of his contemporaries to get the details right. His drawings and
paintings, and particularly his series of sketches of the Newcastle & Carlisle

9

Plate 1.9
London Road Viaduct. *1848*

Railway, provide a valuable source of knowledge for a period when photographs are not available and there is a dependence on artists and illustrators for technical information. Carmichael also conveys the sense of pride and confidence that many had in the new system and its structures at a time when the railway was seen as a symbol of change and progress towards a better world. He may have tried to blend the railway into the landscape but much of his work shows how impossible this proved to be and the strong visual impact that the network began to make on both town and country.

Plate 1.10
Newcastle. *1838*

References

1. Both in the Laing Art Gallery, Newcastle upon Tyne
2. William Bell Scott (1892). Autobiographical Notes, (1), pp 209–210
3. National Railway Museum (NRM) reference: L1F/70R
4. Francis Whishaw (1840). *The Railways of Great Britain and Ireland*
5. Carmichael, J W (1839). *Views on the Newcastle and Carlisle Railway*
6. Tyne and Wear Museums Service (TWCMS) reference: B4824
7. TWCMS: B4833
8. TWCMS: B4832
9. *The Tyne*. This drawing was used on the cover of the six parts of *Views on the Newcastle and Carlisle Railway* which were issued between 1836 and 1838
10. Carlisle Museum and Art Gallery (CMAG) reference: 16–1968–3
11. CMAG: 16–1968–1 and 16–1968–20
12. CMAG: 16–1968–6
13. CMAG: 16–1968–11 and 16–1968–12
14. CMAG: 16–1968–14 and 16–1968–17
15. TWCMS: B6353
16. TWCMS: B6347
17. NRM: 78/21/886 Victoria Bridge over the River Wear
    78/21/973 Willington Dene Viaduct
    78/21/100 Ouseburn Viaduct
18. NRM: 75/21/36
19. NRM: Collection 404 – Railway Infrastructure
20. NRM: 79/21/219
21. *Gateshead Observer*. 1846
22. NRM: Clapham file – Donations (N)
23. NRM: 75/22/42

2 Some observations on Britain's railways and coal

Philip Atkins

The first steam-worked railways evolved in Britain for the conveyance of coal in the early 19th century, since when there has been an intimate, if changing relationship between the railways and the coal industry.

In 1912 about one quarter of all the coal mined in the world was produced in the United Kingdom, whose deposits were unrivalled for quality and whose exports in this commodity dominated the world market. The rate of extraction had increased rapidly throughout the nineteenth century, from only 10 million tons per annum in 1800, to 50 million tons in 1866 and 200 million tons in 1879. Ordinarily 300 million tons would have been reached around 1915 but for the outbreak of World War I during the previous year. Thus what proved to be an all time peak output of 287 million tons was achieved in 1913, the great majority of which would have been moved at some stage by rail, and of which 73 million tons was exported.

In 1900 British sea–borne export coal accounted for eighty–five per cent of the world total but while subsequently continuing to increase in quantity, in actual proportion it had fallen to seventy–one per cent by 1912. Nevertheless, the British contribution, at 67.5 million tons, was well ahead of the amount exported by the nearest competitor, Germany, at 10.3 million tons. The chief markets for British coal were France, Italy, Scandinavia, Germany, Russia, Egypt, Spain, Argentina and Brazil in that order. Best Welsh steam coal was highly prized by several railways in Europe and in Egypt and India, not to mention several foreign navies, on account of its high calorific value and negligible ash content.

In 1913 the movement of coal accounted for nearly £22.7 million, or 19 per cent of the total traffic revenue of the railways in the United Kingdom. On several major railways it accounted for the major single source of freight revenue at a time when *overall* freight movement earned the railways just about twice as much as did passenger traffic. Table 2.1 gives details of the magnitude of and revenue from coal traffic on Britain's railways in the climactic year of 1913.

Plate 2.1
The Midland Railway was the second largest coal haulier after the North Eastern Railway. This March 1905 view of its Wigston, Leics, yard shows a plethora of both railway–owned and privately–owned coal wagons.
Derby Collection/NRM (DY2812)

Table 2.1

Revenue from the Transport of Coal (and Coal Products)
by Railways in the United Kingdom 1913
(from Board of Trade, Annual Railway Returns)

Railway	No of Mineral Wagons	Tonnage tons	Revenue £	Revenue pence (p) per ton
NER	59,815	44,165,950	2,954,300	6.7
GWR	804	37,171,580	2,604,616	7.0
LNWR	9,076	32,784,124	2,365,264	7.2
MR	18,309	31,302,458	3,612,626	11.5
GCR	8,176	23,728,437	1,808,828	7.6
NBR	39,049	20,994,414	1,228,316	5.9
TVR	183	19,392,267	594,753	3.1
LYR	0	15,978,854	981,493	6.1
Cal R	28,604	15,708,040	936,543	6.0
GNR	0	14,197,254	1,280,860	9.0
GER	0	5,078,840	772,266	15.2
G&SWR	11,986	4,861,084	279,701	5.6
LSWR	0	3,612,084	344,808	9.5
SECR	4,790	3,075,389	300,924	9.8
LB&SCR	427	2,137,144	234,822	11.0
Minor	4,385	69,472,217	2,393,754	3.4
Total	**185,704**	**343,660,651**	**22,693,874**	**6.6 (mean)**

Table 2.2

UK Coal Output in 1913

Coalfield	Tonnage	% of total
Northumberland	14,819,328	5.16
Durham	41,532,890	14.45
Yorkshire	43,680,016	15.20
Lancs, Cheshire & N Wales	28,134,364	9.79
Derbys, Notts & Leics	33,702,521	11.73
West Midlands	20,845,761	7.25
South Wales	56,830,317	19.78
Other English*	5,346,239	1.86
Scotland	42,456,516	15.77
	287,347,952	**100.00**

* This would include the new Kent coalfield
which had just commenced production

Although the bulk of the railway network had been completed by, say 1870, the ever increasing output from the mines resulted in the promotion of several new railway projects late in the 19th century, especially to facilitate export to Europe. These were the Hull & Barnsley, Barry and Lancashire, Derbyshire & East Coast railways in the 1880s and 1890s. The LD&ECR was particularly ambitious, being intended to exploit the developing Nottinghamshire and Derbyshire coalfield by spanning England from Warrington (on the new Manchester Ship Canal) to Sutton–on–Sea on the North Sea coast, where a new deep water port was to be built. Involving exceptionally heavy engineering works through the Peak District, only the central section between Chesterfield and Lincoln was ever built and the concern was taken over by the Great Central Railway in 1907. The GCR had already made its own moves to build a major sea port from scratch, at Immingham, which was opened by King George V in July 1912 and which continues to flourish today.

There was plenty of coal for everyone to move and indeed sometimes too much. Late in 1899, at a time of unprecedented demand, the Midland Railway came under fire from Sheffield industrialists through its inability to move coal fast enough from pit to plant. The colliery yards were choked with loaded wagons which the MR had insufficient locomotives to move, a factor exacerbated by severe frost simultaneously dislocating canal traffic (then still important) between Birmingham and Sheffield.

Water–borne coal within and around the UK was indeed very significant. Sailing barges from the North East were already bringing coal to London, particularly for the gas industry, to the tune of around 3 million tons per annum, when the first rail–borne coal, 8377 tons of it, reached the capital over the London & Birmingham Railway in 1845. By 1869 the railways had overtaken coastal shipping and in 1873 attained a peak proportion of sixty–six per cent of the total in this respect. Table 2.3 gives a breakdown by railway for the year 1889 of the carriage of coal to Sherlock Holmes' London.

Table 2.3

Railborne coal to London, 1889

Carrier	tons
Midland Railway	2,647,554
London & North Western Railway	1,735,068
Great Northern Railway	1,360,205
Great Eastern Railway	1,077,504
Great Western Railway	940,829
London & South Western Railway	81,311
South Eastern Railway	27,777
Total by rail	7,870,248
Total by sea	4,767,876
Total by canal	12,602
Grand Total	**12,650,726**

(From *The Railway News*, 14th June 1890)

The pattern was continually changing for by 1898 the advent of the screw barge had tipped the scales once again in favour of the sea–borne trade which, however, temporarily disappeared during World War I owing to the threat of enemy action. In actual amount the maximum tonnage of coal transported by rail to London in peacetime appears to have been 10.1 million tons in 1924. By 1937 this had fallen to only 7 million tons, or only thirty per cent of the record 22.3 million tons brought into London by land and sea during that year.

Transport economics meant that little Welsh coal found its way east to London, but such considerations were transcended by national security during World War I when over 5 million tons of best steam coal were transported by rail *twice* as far *north*. This was conveyed in the so–called Jellicoe Specials to Grangemouth, from whence coasters conveyed it to the Royal Navy's newly established bases in the Cromarty Firth and at Scapa Flow. Remarkably little record of these workings now survives, but such was their intensity that they had to be alternately routed via the East Coast and West Coast main lines. Most of the Navy's warships at that time were coal–fired and the Grand Fleet could consume as much as 100,000 tons of coal during a single week during the course of routine patrols in the North Sea. There is some evidence that in the immediate aftermath of the Agadir Crisis, in 1911, the railways performed several experimental 'dry runs' with train loads of steam coal to the complete satisfaction of the Admiralty.

After World War I the British coal industry confidently anticipated reaching an annual output of 400 million tons and, indeed, the export tonnage initially continued to rise above that for 1913, reaching a peak of 79 million tons in 1923. It thereafter declined largely as a consequence of the Dawes Plan, which was engineered to get Germany back on its economic feet, together with a tendency by European countries to utilize more local coal supplies, albeit of poorer quality, rather than import from Britain. Nevertheless, as late as 1956 the Italian railways were still procuring Welsh steam coal at a time when British Railways were struggling to use coal from Belgium!

Coal was traditionally conveyed on Britain's railways in four–wheeled wooden wagons. From 1887 the latter were built to highly standardized designs to a range of modest capacities (8–15 tons) specified by the Railway Clearing House. These were frequently brightly painted (often brick red or even mustard yellow) and boldly lettered. They served as mobile advertisements for their owners. In 1925 it was estimated that around 700,000 so–called private owner wagons were in use, valued at between £50 and £60 million, or just about half the national wagon total. If one assumes an average length of 19ft 6in over buffers, they would have required something like 2,500 miles of sidings to accommodate them. These wagons were requisitioned by the government during both World Wars and it was estimated that there were still over half a million private owner wagons in service on the formation of British Railways on 1st January 1948, in the immediate aftermath of the nationalization of the British coal industry.

Plate 2.3
North Eastern Railway steel high capacity (32 ton) bogie coal wagon, built in 1902.
York Collection/NRM (YOR 402)

The major main line railways for the most part built remarkably few and in several instances, no mineral wagons at all for the conveyance of coal. A major exception was the North Eastern Railway, which unusually enjoyed a virtual traffic monopoly in its domain and which did not encourage the use of private owner wagons. A progressive railway, from about 1900 it promoted the use of high capacity wagons (of up to 40 tons), sometimes running on bogies, a type which had made comparatively little progress elsewhere even 25 years later. Their advantages were a lower tare weight in relation to carrying capacity, reduced length per ton carried and fewer numbers to couple and uncouple in the yards. Resistance came from the colliery owners on account of their coal screens fouling high–sided wagons, which the GWR attempted to counter by offering a five per cent discount on their rates where entire trains of these wagons were involved, followed by a reduction in tipping and weighing charges at their docks.

The railways charged carriage by weight and distance but, rather like the baker's dozen, for many years they were legally obliged to carry 21 cwt for every ton (of 20 cwt) for which they charged, in order to compensate for loss through residues left in wagons and wind–dispersed dust. This was understandably a serious bone of contention with the railways and in 1896 the statutory ton was reduced to 20½cwt.

Traditionally coal traffic on Britain's railways was worked by inside–cylindered 0–6–0 locomotives, of which several hundred were built during 1899–1901 alone to meet exceptional demand, supplemented by a number of American–built 2–6–0s, particularly on the hard–pressed Midland Railway. From about 1900 increasing numbers of eight–coupled goods locomotives (0–8–0 and 2–8–0) were built and such was the then seemingly boundless year on year increase in coal traffic that in 1914 both the Lancashire & Yorkshire and Great Central railways were actively considering *ten*–coupled engines, ie four–cylinder 2–10–0 and two–cylinder 2–10–2, for the conveyance of coal to their respective East Coast ports at Goole and Immingham.

After 1918 a surplus of 2–8–0s of Great Central design, built for the Railway Operating Division of the Royal Engineers during World War I, depressed the need for new heavy freight locomotives in the early 1920s. Nevertheless the substantial Midlands/South Yorkshire to London coal traffic on the ex–Great Northern and Midland main lines respectively brought forth the two Gresley LNER Class P1 three–cylinder 2–8–2s and 33 LMS 2–6–0 + 0–6–2 Beyer Garratts. These special exceptions apart, which could both handle 100 wagon trains of 1500–1600 tons, G J Churchward's 2–8–0 introduced on the Great Western Railway in 1903 effectively remained as large as anything produced for heavy freight duties until the British Railways Class 9F 2–10–0 was introduced in 1954.

Plate 2.4
London–bound coal. One of the two Gresley LNER Class P1 2–8–2 heavy coal locomotives built in 1925 (No. 2393) hauls an up 100 wagon coal train at Sandy on 8th June 1933. The auxiliary booster was still fitted to the hind–truck of the engine at this date and was possibly in operation at the moment the exposure was made.
G H Soole Collection/NRM (GHS 168)

In their steam locomotives the railways were major consumers of coal. In their early years they were obliged, on what would now be termed environmental grounds, to burn smokeless coke, an expensive commodity, but from about 1870 following the perfection of the firebrick arch on the Midland Railway coal fuel became feasible. During the period 1900–1950 around 20,000 plus steam locomotives consumed 12–13 million tons of coal per annum. An article in *The Railway Magazine* for September 1901 went to elaborate lengths to convey to the reader the sheer bulk of the coal then consumed each year by Britain's railways, eg a coal train stretching 600 miles from Birmingham to Constantinople (Istanbul), or a tender (water excluded) which would have measured 2000 ft long, by 333 ft wide and 404 ft high!

Having said all this the railways actually consumed appreciably less coal than did the coal industry itself and were well down the national league table. Table 2.4 gives the position as it was in 1903, when the then embryonic electricity generating industry was not even mentioned. By the 1970s it would be the largest single consumer. It is also interesting to note that in the early 20th century it was estimated that no less than twenty per cent of the coal mined in the United States was burnt in locomotive fireboxes (and there were appreciable numbers of oil and wood burning locomotives in service there at that time).

Table 2.4

Coal Consumption in the United Kingdom, 1903 – A Breakdown

	million tons
Factories	53
Domestic consumers	32
Iron & steel industry	28
Mines	18
Gas industry	15
Railways	13
Bricks, glass, potteries & chemical plants	5
Other	1
Total	**167**

Prior to 1914, commodity prices, including that of coal, fluctuated considerably despite low rates of monetary inflation. In times of industrial boom, ie the early 1870s, early 1890s, 1899–1900 and around 1907, the price markedly rose. In times of economic depression, eg the 1880s, it was notably low. As a rule of thumb it was reckoned fuel costs normally accounted for roughly twenty–five per cent of the railways' operating costs and a price change could markedly influence their profitability and so the dividend paid to their shareholders.

Plate 2.5
Stockpiles of locomotive coal at
Whitemoor Depot, Great Eastern
Railway, during the Coal Strike
of 1912.
*Stratford Collection/NRM (SX
992)*

Most railways negotiated contracts on a 6–month basis with the coal owners at
the end and middle of each year. The pace–setter, however, was the mighty North
Eastern Railway, the greatest coal haulier of them all, which negotiated for a
12–month period after Christmas at Barnsley, which by the later 19th century was
the coal capital of Britain. The other railways closely watched the outcome of the
NER negotiations.

In 1873, following a substantial (sixty–two per cent) pay award secured by the
miners, the price of coal nearly doubled and stood as high as 14s (70p) per ton,
but by 1880 it had fallen below 6s (30p). It fluctuated only slightly during the
1880s but by 1890 had reached around 9s (45p). Demand by industry at the close
of the century was well nigh insatiable. In June 1899 the price was set at 10s 6d
(52p), but soon there was talk of a possible coal famine and in June 1900 the
GER and LYR both agreed to 16s (80p). In a coal–based industrial economy
such a price increase must have appeared every bit as devastating as the oil price
increases of late 1973 in our own time. In fact the price of coal soon declined
again as is reflected in Table 2.5. During World War I there were sharp
inflationary increases in price and by 1917–1918 acute shortages forced a
reduction in passenger train services and the rationalization of them by formerly
rival companies in a given region in the national interest. In the immediate
post–war period coal for locomotive purposes was actually being imported from
such countries as Poland and resulted, in 1920, in experiments with oil burning on
the London & North Western and Highland railways.

Table 2.5

Locomotive Coal cost per ton, MR 1873–1896 and LNWR 1895–1922

MR

	Pence per ton			Pence per ton
1873	72.0		1885	32.7
1874	72.0		1886	31.25
1875	53.5		1887	30.0
1876	46.0		1888	30.5
1877	38.5		1889	35.3
1878	33.0		1890	45.6
1879	30.0		1891	47.9
1880	29.0		1892	46.0
1881	30.0		1893*	52.25
1882	30.3		1894	41.1
1883	32.3		1895	39.0
1884	34.2		1896	35.1

LNWR

	Jan–Jun	Jul–Dec		Jan–Jun	Jul–Dec
	Pence per ton			Pence per ton	
1895	36.0	34.6	1909	58.1	53.3
1896	33.8	32.4	1910	52.5	52.2
1897	31.9	31.9	1911	51.8	53.1
1898	31.9	33.8	1912	53.4	50.7
1899	35.5	39.4	1913	54.2	60.1
1900	36.6	58.5	1914	60.3	59.2
1901	63.7	46.9	1915+	61.0	82.3
1902	45.9	42.6	1916+	83.6	85.4
1903	42.4	42.8	1917+	91.6	93.6
1904	42.8	42.2	1918+	101.5	109.4
1905	42.5	50.7	1919	126.0	138.4
1906	51.0	50.0	1920	173.5	188.8
1907	50.8	66.7	1921	240.0	215.0
1908	54.6	57.7	1922	132.7	105.4

* Coal strike
+ World War I

The GNR, GER and LNWR each imported coal from Belgium during the four–month strike by the miners in 1893 but experienced great difficulty with it, with some trains coming to a standstill. This prompted the GER to experiment with using the unpleasant oil–residue from its plant producing gas for carriage lighting purposes. For quite a few years a number of its passenger locomotives ran as oil–burners and it was only the conversion to electric lighting that brought this interesting development to an end. When the miners commenced serious wage negotiations with the coal owners in the autumn of 1911, the GER immediately began to stockpile 120,000 tons of coal at Whitemoor and it was *not* amongst the lines, which included the Midland and Caledonian, that resorted to oil–firing during the 1912 coal strike. Oil burning made a token appearance again during the 1921 and 1926 strikes, and amid chronic shortages after World War II, an ambitious government scheme to convert over 1200 locomotives was initiated in 1947. Except on the GWR, this was largely overtaken by events and only a fraction of the engines scheduled were actually converted. After 1939 good quality locomotive coal could not always be guaranteed and in the post–war years its quality continued to decline whilst its cost steadily increased. By 1957 the situation was such and the cost of oil so relatively low (despite the recent Suez Crisis) that what was now the Western Region of British Railways seriously considered equipping some steam locomotives for oil firing once again.

The fundamental decision to abandon steam traction on British Railways had already been taken in late 1954, after there had been a further sharp increase in the cost of coal. There had been growing concern over the escalating cost, and simultaneously the declining availability and quality of locomotive fuel since the end of World War II, coupled with concern as to atmospheric pollution. The decision when announced in January 1955, was by no means unexpected, having come later rather than sooner.

The portents were there as long ago as the eve of World War I when the steam locomotive still ruled supreme. In 1911 concern developed that at the then current rate of extraction British coal deposits would become depleted in less than 200 years. *The Railway Gazette* (for 15th September) prophetically commented that "it is quite possible that before the time limit put upon the continuation of the coal supply has expired, the steam–actuated railway engine may have been relegated to the limbo of forgotten inventions and another more potent type of motor will have taken its place". Only six months later in March 1912 one Dr Rudolph Diesel addressed the Institution of Mechanical Engineers and remarked "whether a Diesel locomotive can be made a practical commercial success remains to be seen, but there can be no doubt that no effort will be spared to make it work".

The good doctor did not live to witness the worldwide railway motive power revolution that would bear his name take place. Now in Britain the steam locomotives of yesteryear have long gone, but highly sophisticated diesel–electric locomotives haul long block trains of close–coupled hopper waggons conveying coal from pit head to power station in the non–stop "merry go round" trains, inaugurated in 1965 which earn British Rail a substantial proportion of its annual revenue.

Plate 2.7
A British Railways Class 56 Co–Co diesel electric locomotive hauls a train of hopper wagons comprising a 'Merry Go Round' unit near Didcot in June 1979.
T E Williams Collection/NRM (TEW 11621)

3 Nineteenth century production and pricing at Beyer, Peacock & Company, Locomotive Manufacturers, Manchester

Christine J Heap

Charles Babbage writing *On the Economy of Machinery and Manufactures* in 1832 stated,

> "The first object of every person who attempts to make an article of consumption is, or ought to be, to produce it in perfect form, but in order to secure to himself the greatest and most permanent profit, he must endeavour by every means in his power to render the new luxury or want which he has created, cheap to those who consume it. He must carefully arrange the whole system of his factory in such a manner that the article he sells to the public may be produced at as small a cost as possible".[1]

Sydney Pollard writing in the 1960s identified the first need of industrial enterprises as

> "The achievement of some order so that control could become rational and purposeful".[2]

The question of costing and pricing in industry during the eighteenth and nineteenth centuries has exercised the minds of historians in recent years in connection with the growth of managerial control of industrial production. As industrial production became increasingly complex the industrial entrepreneur had to keep track of an ever increasing number of elements bearing on his business such as capital investment, factory rents, plant renewal, raw material costs, labour costs, market demands, work flow and production rate. All these elements created an imperative need for a technique of control that would enable the manufacturer to keep track of his resources and to direct his production towards the achievement of his plans. What the entrepreneur needs to know for the success of his business sounds simple enough. He must know the likely demand for his product, the costs involved in producing his product and the price he must charge for his product in order to stay in business.

This paper will look briefly at the order and control established in the locomotive manufacturing business of Beyer, Peacock & Company, between the years 1854 when the company was founded and 1902 when it became a public limited company. The paper will look at work–flow and factory organisation and examine Beyer, Peacock's costing and pricing of products. The two aspects are obviously linked and both are concerned with the manufacturer's endeavours to secure to himself the "greatest and most permanent profit".

Beyer, Peacock & Company, locomotive manufacturers of Gorton, Manchester was founded in 1854, by Charles Beyer, Richard Peacock and Henry Robertson. The first partnership agreement between these three, drawn up in 1855, specified the business of the firm to be that of Mechanical Engineers and to be confined chiefly to the manufacture of locomotive engines.[3] Each partner was to contribute £10,000 to the undertaking. The Company's first minute book indicates that during January 1855, Beyer paid £9,524–10–0, Peacock £5,500 and Robertson £4,000 into the Company.[4] All three partners had previous experience of the locomotive and railway business and business accounting which no doubt stood them in good stead in founding their new enterprise.

Plate 3.1
Charles Frederick Beyer (1813–1876) born in Plauen, Saxony and co–founder of the locomotive manufacturing concern which bore his name Beyer, Peacock & Company, Gorton, Manchester.

Plate 3.2
Richard Peacock (1820–1889) born in Swaledale, Yorkshire was the locomotive superintendent of the Manchester, Sheffield & Lincolnshire Railway before joining Beyer to found Beyer, Peacock & Company.

Charles Beyer, educated at Dresden Polytechnic from 1828–1832 had some knowledge of book–keeping practices both from his college course where he was required to study book–keeping and from his later employment at Sharp Roberts & Company. In fact Beyer brought one of Sharp Robert's cost–of–work books with him when he founded Beyer, Peacock.[5] Richard Peacock had worked as locomotive superintendent on the Manchester, Sheffield & Lincolnshire Railway in a department where a number of clerks were employed keeping records of large scale financial transactions.[6] Henry Robertson had worked with Robert Stephenson and Joseph Locke in building railway lines and letting contracts and later had bought and developed the Brymbo Iron & Steel Company in Wales.[7] With this experience behind them, how did Beyer, Peacock and Robertson tackle the problem of production, costing and pricing in their locomotive business in order to ensure, in Babbage's words, the goods they made were produced in perfect form but at as small a cost as possible?

Firstly, they made sure that the site chosen for the factory had definite economic advantages. Beyer, Peacock's site was at Gorton, two miles from Manchester city

Plate 3.3
Henry Robertson (1816–1888) born at Banff in Scotland. He was the third partner in the firm Beyer, Peacock & Company.

centre. This was considered a good position in view of the facility with which materials could be procured and workmen engaged. In Richard Peacock's words, Gorton was "near enough to Manchester to get the benefits therefrom but far enough out to escape the heavy local taxes with which such establishments in town were burdened".[8] The siting of the manufacturing enterprises in areas where costs could be kept down was not of course new. Boulton and Watt had chosen a site adjacent to a canal for their Soho foundry to ease transport of castings to and from the works.[9] James Nasmyth had similarly sited the Bridgewater Foundry near both the Bridgewater canal and the Liverpool & Manchester Railway[10] and of course Richard Peacock had chosen Gorton for the site of the Manchester, Sheffield & Lincolnshire Railway workshops.[11] The experience of the old Manchester firm of Sharp Roberts illustrates the economic importance of factory location. Sharp Roberts in 1888 decided to move from Manchester largely because of the increasing costs of rates, taxes and ground rents payable on enterprises in the city, because of the heavy cost of carriage from the works to the nearest railway station and the higher rate of wages which had to be paid in Manchester.[12]

Secondly, Beyer's arranged the manufacturing so that a logical workflow was possible. Beyer himself seems to have been responsible for the design of the factory and obviously took great care over its layout. It was a great boast of Gorton Foundry that not a single workshop as originally laid out had had to be pulled down in the process of extension. Throughout its life, although greatly extended, Gorton Foundry retained the same basic order of shops.[13] From the drawing office, the drawings for locomotives would proceed to the pattern shop for the appropriate patterns to be made. These would then proceed to the iron and brass foundries as appropriate. From there a large proportion of the work would go to the smithy to be further finished. Here such items as reversing and brake shafts, valve buckles, bogie spring beams and firebox rings were built up before proceeding to the machine shops.

Plate 3.4
The turning shop at Beyer, Peacock & Company Ltd. Here the wheels were finished, forced on their axles and tyred. The photograph was taken about 1904.

25

Other items such as the cylinders, wheels and all brasswork cast in the respective foundries would cross the yard to the machine shops to be examined, bored and planed as appropriate. They would then proceed to the fitting shops to be fitted to the locomotive frames. Components for the boiler would be taken from the foundry through to the boiler shops where some machining would be carried out and the foundation rings and boiler plates rivetted. From there the boiler would be taken to the fitting shops for valves, cocks and other items to be fitted before arriving in the erecting shops where the whole would come together. The primary aim of the layout was no doubt that of reducing the amount of handling required of heavy and large components but it also resulted in the establishment of a logical sequence and flow of events. The same pattern was apparent at Nasmyth's locomotive works where the shops were said to be all in a line and the work proceeded logically from one operation to the next, and at the other locomotive manufacturers' works such as Dübs and Neilsons in Glasgow.[14]

Thirdly, although there was still a large amount of hand–forging, smithing and hand–fitting, as revealed by the number of men employed in these categories, Beyer, Peacock also invested quite heavily in modern machine tools and were quite prepared to innovate where appropriate to overcome difficulties in production. Beyer and Molyneaux in 1864, noting deficiencies in a wheel lathe bought from William Collier developed their own version in which the headstock and face–plate were considerably heavier in proportion than the corresponding part of the Collier lathe.[15] Beyer himself produced a drilling and boring machine in which three drilling heads operating together made it easier to drill holes in a straight line.[16] Later Richard Peacock noting how time consuming was the process of hand lapping required to correct inaccuracies in steel parts, due to distortion during case–hardening, developed his planetary grinding spindle in 1887. By the introduction of this type of grinding spindle, the correction of inaccuracies in steel details became a simple matter of machine operation considerably reducing the time taken to produce a satisfactory job.[17] In order to keep abreast of modern developments Beyer, Peacock introduced hydraulic rivetting in 1879,[18] electric lighting in 1887 and electric driving for the work's machinery in 1897-1904,[19] but all was done without any cost analysis of the proposed improvements either before or after their introduction. Ralph Peacock is said to have made exhaustive enquiries into electric driving abroad before introducing it to Gorton[20] but no record of his findings survives to show whether possible cost savings were reviewed or not. It could be that the situation was still as Pollard described it for the earlier part of the century when new techniques were so obviously better it did not need elaborate accounts to prove them so.

Fourthly, Beyer, Peacock like most of the other engineering works of the time, made extensive use of measuring machines, templates and gauges, so that, in the words of the correspondent from the Engineer who visited the works in 1856, "the workmen can proceed to finish separate pieces of the same engine with thorough confidence that when they are brought together the fit will be accurate".[21] By keeping all their old drawings and patterns, Beyer's also ensured that duplicate parts for an engine could be made with the minimum amount of fuss and delay and the maximum amount of profit.

The result of these four factors of organisation was that Beyer's were able to maintain their productive efficiency throughout the period under review, ie from the 1850s to 1900. Assessing the productive efficiency of a nineteenth century locomotive builder is, however, no easy task. The number of locomotives produced per year is no indication of productive capacity or efficiency; so many factors including the prevailing economic climate, continental wars and competition affect the picture. Taking one of Beyer, Peacock's own measures of productive efficiency, the length of time required to produce a locomotive from the completion of the drawing office order to the delivery of the first engine, it seems that Beyer's managed to maintain the time for many of its orders at between three and four months throughout its first fifty years. Beyer himself in 1863 had said he could deliver any kind of engine, *"providing they are our scheme in $3\frac{1}{2}$ months"*.[22]

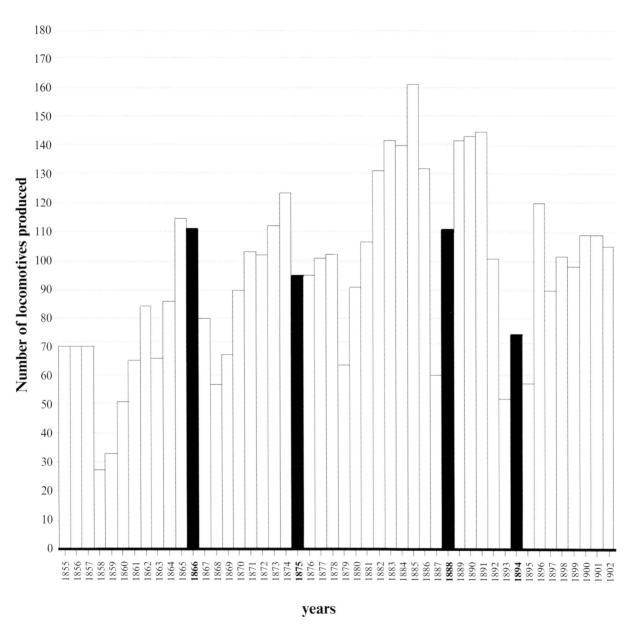

Table 3.1

In 1866 the Norwegian 2–4–0 tank locomotive (order number 2000) weighing fourteen tons, took three months ten days to construct. In 1875 an 0–6–0 tank for the Gefle–Dala Railway, weighing twenty–seven tons (order number 3288) took four months sixteen days: an 0–6–2 tank for the La Guaira & Caracas Railway, in 1888 took four months five days and in 1904 the 4–4–2 tender engine for the Great Central Railway weighing sixty–three tons (locomotive alone) four months fourteen days.[23] In spite of increasing boiler capacity, greater number of tubes, greater number of wheels from six to eight to ten, with corresponding increases in the work on frames, axleforks, cheekblocks, axle–boxes and spring fittings, the delivery times remained more or less constant. The block graph in Table 3.1 shows the number of engines produced each year; none of the selected examples are from years when the works were particularly slack.

Behind this production stood an army of clerical workers whose job it was to compile the detailed records of costs which were necessary for the firm to know how much it should be charging for its work and if it was making a profit. On commencing business in 1854 Beyer, Peacock almost immediately employed an accountant cashier, Edwin James Webb, who joined the company on 2 August 1854 at a wage of £2.10.0d a week. This remuneration compared favourably with the draughtsmen's wages for the same month of between £1.5s.0s. and £3.0s.0d. a week and the foreman's wages of £2.0s.0d to £5.0s.0d a week.[24] Within the next ten years Webb's salary had increased to £6.0s.0d. equalling that of the leading foreman and the head draughtsman.[25] By March 1866, Beyer's were employing 33 clerks, office workers and time–keepers against 15 foremen, 26 draughtsmen, 61 forgemen and 1,451 workmen – a ratio of one clerk to 57 other employees.[26] By 1890 the ratio was one clerk to thirty–five other employees.[27]

This is in stark contrast to the practice at Hawthorn Leslie's where the pricing of locomotives was by no means successful and William Cross who joined the firm in 1882 had cause to complain of the lack of accurate cost books and suggested that it might not be a bad idea to appoint one or two clerks to keep accurate records.[28]

The task of the clerks employed by Beyer's and other locomotive manufacturers can to some extent be judged by the books they were required to keep. Even though few of the books themselves have survived, lists of them usually appear in the company's inventory. There is a list in Henry Dübs inventory for 1865 which gives the following: ledgers, journal, cashbook, billbook, private ledger, balance book, salaries book, two wage books, iron and brass foundry day books, two cost books, buildings and tools book, invoice and price list books, inward and outward order books, goods received and delivered books, two time ledgers, one abstract and two check books, six time survey and one piece contract book, register of drawings, register of specifications, three letter copy books and three order books.[29] Similar books were kept by Beyer's of which the ledgers, cash books, wage books, wage abstract books, buildings and tool book (which is actually the inventory), register of drawings, order books and cost of work books survive. The wage analysis books and the cost of work books were possibly the two most important books for the cost accounting side of the business – being concerned with the proportion of cost in terms of wages, materials, overheads, etc., accruing to each locomotive order. The wage analysis book shows the cost in terms of wages allocated to each order.

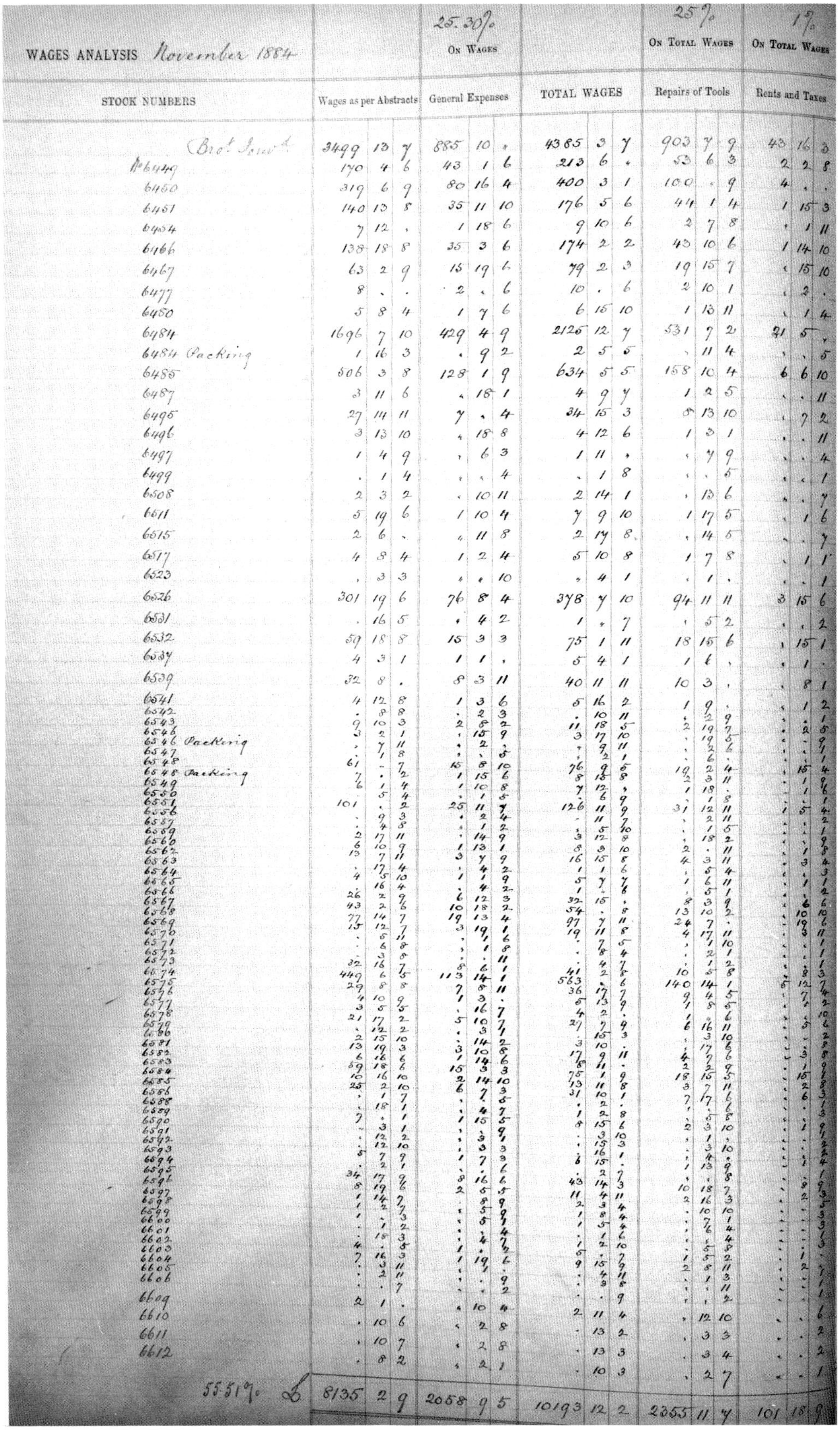

STOCK NUMBERS	Wages as per Abstracts			General Expenses (25.30% On Wages)			TOTAL WAGES			Repairs of Tools (25% On Total Wages)			Rents and Taxes (1% On Total Wages)		
Brot. forwd.	3499	13	7	885	10	.	4385	3	7	903	7	9	43	16	3
No 6449	170	4	6	43	1	6	213	6	.	53	6	3	2	2	8
6450	319	6	9	80	16	4	400	3	1	100	.	9	4	.	.
6451	140	13	8	35	11	10	176	5	6	44	1	4	1	15	3
6454	7	12	.	1	18	6	9	10	6	2	7	8	.	1	11
6466	138	18	8	35	3	6	174	2	2	43	10	6	1	14	10
6467	63	2	9	15	19	6	79	2	3	19	15	7	.	15	10
6477	8	.	.	2	.	6	10	.	6	2	10	1	.	2	.
6480	5	8	4	1	7	6	6	15	10	1	13	11	.	1	4
6484	1696	7	10	429	4	9	2125	12	7	531	7	2	21	5	.
6484 Packing	1	16	3	.	9	2	2	5	5	.	11	4	.	.	5
6485	506	3	8	128	1	9	634	5	5	158	10	4	6	6	10
6487	3	11	6	.	18	1	4	9	7	1	2	5	.	.	11
6495	27	14	11	7	.	4	34	15	3	8	13	10	.	7	2
6496	3	13	10	.	18	8	4	12	6	1	3	1	.	.	11
6497	1	4	9	.	6	3	1	11	.	.	7	9	.	.	4
6499	.	1	4	.	.	4	.	1	8	.	.	5	.	.	1
6508	2	3	2	.	10	11	2	14	1	.	13	6	.	.	7
6511	5	19	6	1	10	4	7	9	10	1	17	5	.	1	6
6515	2	6	.	.	11	8	2	17	8	.	14	5	.	.	7
6517	4	8	4	1	2	4	5	10	8	1	7	8	.	1	1
6523	.	3	3	.	.	10	.	4	1	.	1	.	.	.	1
6526	301	19	6	76	8	4	378	7	10	94	11	11	3	15	6
6531	.	16	5	.	4	2	1	.	7	.	5	2	.	.	2
6532	59	18	8	15	3	3	75	1	11	18	15	6	.	15	1
6537	4	3	1	1	1	.	5	4	1	1	6	.	.	1	.
6539	32	8	.	8	3	11	40	11	11	10	3	.	.	8	1
6541	4	12	8	1	3	6	5	16	2	1	9	.	.	1	2
55.51%	8135	2	9	2058	9	5	10193	12	2	2355	11	7	101	18	9

Plate 3.5
A page from the Beyer, Peacock Wage Analysis Book for 1884 showing the allocation of wages and general expenses for orders worked on during November 1884. Order number 6595, two 2–6–0 tender engines for the Western Australian Government Railway detailed in Table 3.3, appears towards the bottom of the page.

The information about wages was gathered from the workmen themselves via the time clerk. To glean this vital information every workman (except labourers) had to give in the particulars of what he had been working at during each day and if he had worked on more than one job he was required to give in the exact time he was at each job.

Table 3.2
Draughtsmen's time charged to Order Number 2159

Year	Draughtsmen *(See Key below)*											
1867	**1**	**2**	**3**	**4**	**5**	**6**	**7**	**8**	**9**	**10**	**11**	**12**
Months	**Hours worked on this order**											
June	172				91	46		74	33		51	
July		177	51	158	211	194	167	182	150	228	150	
August	16	45	27					19	19	19	18	19
Sept									9			
Oct	4			4								
Total	192	223	78	163	303	240	167	275	211	247	220	19

Total hours   2,338
Total Wages   £92–7s–9d

Draughtsmen
        1 = Peacock, **2** = Fox, **3** = Swift, **4** = Schmidt, **5** = Glen,
        6 = Shaw, **7** = Struve, **8** = Gorstling, **9** = Green,
        10 = Gluns, **11** = Hayes, **12** = Tipping

*Note: Fractions in the hours worked have been omitted and the total rounded up where appropriate.

Table 3.2 shows how one department, in this case the drawing office, allocated time and therefore wages to one order. In addition labourer's wages, manager's salaries, foremen's wages, clerks salaries, and unspecified items termed general charges were added together, under the heading General Expenses and allocated as a percentage over the orders completed in that month. Likewise rents, taxes and repairs of tools were added on a percentage basis.[30] This represented Beyer, Peacock's attempts at allocating overhead charges. Table 3.3 shows how the system worked over one locomotive order.

Similar detailed records were kept of the materials used on each locomotive order.[31] For each order a breakdown of materials by weight required, and their current price is given. In addition to these books recording information by locomotive, Dübs, Neilson and possibly Beyer too, kept detail cost books recording the costs of various components required for each order. These books recorded in detail the costs of material going into boilers, fireboxes, grates, axleboxes, engine nameplates, etc. Dübs kept eleven of these detail cost books.

Table 3.3

Wages allocated to Order Number 6595, Two 2-6-0 Tender Engines for the Western Australian Government Railway, [from Beyer, Peacock Wages Analysis Book 3]

October 1884	Wages	£ 4. 2. 0	
	General Expenses	£ .19. 3	25.58% on wages
	Repairs	£ 1. 1. 3	21% on wages + G.E.
	Rents & Taxes	£ . 1. 0	1% on wages + G.E.
November 1884	Wages	£ 34.17. 9	
	General Expenses	£ 8.16. 6	25.30% on wages
	Repairs	£ 10.18. 7	25% on wages + G.E.
	Rents & Taxes	£ . 8. 9	1% on wages + G.E.
December 1884	Wages	£ 89. 3.11	
	General Expenses	£ 24. 0. 7	26.93% on wages
	Repairs	£ 28. 6. 2	25% on wages + G.E.
	Rates & Taxes	£ 2. 5. 3	2% on wages + G.E.
January 1885	Wages	£103.13. 5	
	General Expenses	£ 28.14.10	27.7% on wages
	Repairs	£ 26. 9. 8	20% on wages + G.E.
	Rates & Taxes	£ 2. 2.11	2% on wages + G.E.
February 1885	Wages	£ 74.13. 4	
	General Expenses	£ 18. 4. 4	24.4% on wages
	Repairs	£ 20. 8. 8	22% on wages + G.E.
	Rates + Taxes	£ 1.17. 2	2% on wages + G.E.
March 1885	Wages	£212. 3. 0	
	General Expenses	£ 53.12. 7	25.28% on wages
	Repairs	£ 53. 3. 1	20% on wages + G.E.
	Rates & Taxes	£ 5. 6. 3	2% on wages + G.E.
April 1885	Wages	£ 66. 3. 2	
	General Expenses	£ 19.11. 4	29.57% on wages
	Repairs	£ 21. 8. 5	25% on wages + G.E.
	Rates & Taxes	£ 1.14. 3	2% on wages + G.E.
May 1885	Wages	£ 18. 0. 1	
	General Expenses	£ 5.12. 8	31.28% on wages
	Repairs	£ 5.18. 2	25% on wages + G.E.
	Rates & Taxes	£ . 9. 5	2% on wages + G.E.
June 1885	Wages	£ . . 2	
	General Expenses	£ . . 1	
	Repairs	£ . . 1	
	Rates & Taxes	£ . . 1	
Totals	Wages	£602.16. 9	
	General Expenses	£159.10.11	
	Repairs of Tools	£167.14. 1	
	Rates & Taxes	£ 14. 5. 1	

These details correspond with the details given in the cost of work book as follows:
Wages £600. General Expenses £159. Gas, Coke, Coal/ Rates & Taxes/ Repairs of Tools £211.11. 5. The wages and General Expenses have been rounded down. Rents & Taxes and Repairs of Tools have been added together giving £181.19. 2 plus £30 for gas, coke and coal. With the cost of materials the locomotives cost ex works £1,987.8.1 or £993.14.0 each. With tender £2,358.16.5 or £1,179.8.2 each. They were sold for £3,500 or £1,750 each.

By keeping two sets of records it was possible for the locomotive manufacturer to check probable costs for either various locomotive components in the detail cost books or various locomotive types in the locomotive cost books. When an enquiry was received from a railway company or industrial concern for an estimate for a new locomotive, the first task would be to look at the design of the engine and by breaking the order down into constituent parts compare with any similar locomotive built at the works. The more nearly a locomotive approximated another, the more accurate the estimate could hope to be and the less time was required for the design stage. The more different the design, the more difficult the task of estimating the cost of production and the longer the design stage.

One hundred consecutive locomotive orders received by Beyer, Peacock between 1869 and 1874 can be used to show the effects on profit of using previous designs.[32] Of the one hundred orders, 62 were repeated designs of which 49 gave over 25% profit and 0 less than 15% profit; 38 were new designs of which only 10 gave over 25% profit and 16 less than 15% profit.[32] There was therefore a great incentive for the manufacturer to steer customers towards previous designs. Unfortunately, there were also a number of factors militating against the use of standard designs on anything like a large scale. A worldwide market meant several different gauges of track from 2ft. to 5ft. 6ins. The gradients and radii of the curves on the railway networks varied considerably; wayside and overline structures determined the width and height of locomotives which could be used. Each country developed its own safety regulations which had to be adhered to and different locomotive engineers had different ideas on the best locomotive design. In spite of these difficulties, the private builders did what they could to promote previous designs by personal influence and by issuing their agents with illustrated catalogues of successful types.[33] Not only did they stand to make more profit by doing so but they could save tremendously on the time required for design work.

Locomotives based on previous designs were much easier to produce to drawing office order stage. As an example, a Norwegian 2–4–0 Tank locomotive, (order number 2000), took fourteen months to design[34] (Plate 3.6). From receipt of the initial enquiry in March 1865 to the issue of the complete drawing office order fourteen months elapsed.

Plate 3. 6
The Norwegian Government Railway 2–4–0 tank locomotive, No 2, *Tryccve*, ordered in 1866. (*Beyer, Peacock Order No. 2000*)

By contrast, the Isle of Man 2–4–0 Tank engines (order number 2965) based on the earlier Norwegian design took only six months to design[35] (Plate 3.7). In both cases from the issue of the complete drawing office order to the delivery of the first locomotive, around three and a half months elapsed.

Plate 3.7
The Isle of Man Railway 2–4–0 tank locomotive, No 1, *Sutherland*, ordered in 1872 *(Beyer, Peacock Order No 2965)* and based on the earlier Norwegian Government locomotive design. *(Beyer, Peacock Order No 2000).*

Once a locomotive was defined in terms of design, the next stage was to estimate the cost of material required. This was more difficult than it might at first seem because not only did different railway companies often require metals from different iron manufacturers, which meant different rates and costs, but the costs of the same firm's product could fluctuate widely. This was partly due to external factors such as the international situation, peace or war and the level of investment, and partly due to the system of marketing metals which allowed speculators to buy and store pig iron and copper until a high price could be obtained. As Beyer,Peacock usually worked to fixed price contracts the importance of correctly gauging the state of the metal market and the trend in prices cannot be overstated. It also underlines the necessity of completing an order as quickly as possible. As the Managing Director of the Madras Railway so clearly understood in a letter of 1854

> "Owing to the continued rise in price of copper, iron plate etc., the parties tendering are anxious to secure an answer as soon as possible".[36]

An examination of Beyer, Peacock's cost of work books shows that locomotive selling prices broadly follow the trends in material prices, being lower during the periods of low material costs.

But this is not the whole story because in addition to the design factors and material costs, market factors also influenced the pricing of a locomotive. If competition was fierce or the customers particularly desired, a large discount could be offered, in Beyer's case up to 20% off the quoted price. Beyer, Peacock's instructions to their Australian agent W.S. Brewster make this quite clear:

> "It must be understood that the full prices are to be quoted and obtained where possible, but in cases of severe competition to be contended with they may be reduced 2%, 5%, 7% or even 10%".[37]

Writing further in 1887 Beyer, Peacock said,

> "We have decided to increase the discounts all round and until further notice you may act on the following rule, namely: List price less 15% with extra margin of 2% or if necessary up to 5% making a total of 20% to be taken off in cases of severe competition".[38]

Having signed a contract for a locomotive Beyer, Peacock would construct it as best it could within the estimate, keeping detailed record costs for future reference. The figures were retrospective however – in other words they were not available quickly enough to enable immediate comparisons between actual and estimated costs to be made. Only when it was too late to make adjustments did Beyer discover whether they had made a profit on the particular order concerned. The necessary figures however were available for consultation when another similar order came in. At the end of the year the figures were also available for that year's trading to show the overall profitability of the concern.

Beyer, Peacock in the nineteenth century was obviously a profitable concern as shown by the profits declared by them from their foundation to 1882 *(See Table 3.4)*. These figures must be treated with some caution however:

a) because they are percentage figures of cumulative Capital (ie the total sum of money invested in the company over the years) and

b) because there is no depreciation allowance against them.

Nevertheless they are quite an impressive set of returns and even when adjusted for depreciation and expressed as a percentage of capital employed in the modern sense, i.e. net tangible assets less liabilities, the profits compare reasonably well with those declared by companies in the mid twentieth century.

Table 3.4
Beyer, Peacock Declared Profits

	Net Profits in £–s–d	Profits as % on cost of work	Capital Expended Cumulative Total in £–s–d	Profit as % on capital expended
1854			23,643.10.02	
1855	2,504.01.07	43.44	41,843.01.09	5.98
1856	7,136.01.07	8.31	47,086.13.06	15.15
1857	11,508.17.05	10.90	56,042.16.04	20.53
1858	24,015.17.10	23.04	67,270.05.04	35.70
1859	21,670.08.02	23.83	71,185.18.08	30.44
1860	20,810.14.02	20.38	86,506.00.05	24.05
1861	32,770.02.01	20.71	107,640.08.08	30.44
1862	27,346.13.01	32.82	120,250.15.02	22.74
1863	85,761.16.07	35.32	124,292.05.06	69.00
1864	75,576.01.00	32.44	139,898.14.07	53.87
1865	80,704.13.10	30.91	175,944.19.03	45.30
1866	74,969.18.10	31.27	191,240.01.04	39.20
1867	60,019.04.06	31.26	193,335.19.02	31.04
1868	38,622.08.02	31.03	194,520.08.06	19.85
1869	47,720.08.04	25.04	197,177.13.06	24.20
1870	45,659.04.00	19.01	198,312.06.08	23.02
1871	54,892.14.02	29.93	202,521.14.07	27.10
1872	57,005.01.02	21.52	203,241.09.02	28.04
1873	82,381.08.02	26.24	208,120.10.03	39.58
1874	75,022.13.11	26.03	216,612.15.02	34.63
1875	54,738.02.08	25.14	218,846.07.05	25.01
1876	43,323.16.10	21.18	218,957.15.05	19.85
1877	48,908.05.10	20.72	218,997.18.08	22.33
1878	40,631.18.04	17.68	219,868.04.11	18.49
1879	12,090.13.02	8.77	226,263.13.11	5.34
1880	28,016.02.03	14.10	231,695.07.00	12.09
1881	24,893.07.07	13.27	236,575.04.09	10.52
1882	34,203.06.08	9.34	245,127.12.03	13.95

Total amount of Bad Debts: £2846.15.00

Looking at the business organisation of Beyer, Peacock & Company in the nineteenth century, it is clear that, in the siting and layout of the factory, in the adoption of strict procedures for collecting accounting information and in their attempt to deal with some of the major costing problems of the nineteenth century such as the allocation of overhead costs, Beyer, Peacock were making reasonable efforts to run their business economically and efficiently. It is also clear however that there were limits to what could be achieved. Necessity proved itself a large limiting factor. Unless there was a perceived need to re–examine production techniques or to tighten up on financial control there was no incentive to do so.

There is no evidence to suggest that Beyer, Peacock knew what its break–even point was, ie how many locomotives or machine tools it had to sell at what price in order to cover its costs. The question of unused plant capacity and how best to account for it was not addressed. There was little immediate control of production costs to enable adjustments to the building programme to be made and more seriously there was no attempt at depreciating the fixed assets. It is interesting to speculate whether the refusal to set up a depreciation fund was a deliberate ploy to ensure that the future of the company remained firmly in the hands of the partners. Whilst this was the case, the partners were the ones who were called upon to provide additional money for plant renewal and they could refuse or agree to provide that money at will. This could also give the partners a lever in any negotiations with the unions. Machines which aimed to speed up production and therefore promised to "curb trade unions with more labour saving machinery"[39] could be renewed at any time or not as the partners willed without having to be accounted to a depreciation fund. Whatever the truth of this speculation it is interesting to note that it was not until after the arrival of the Public Limited Company in 1902 that a depreciation fund was established at Beyer, Peacock's.

Beyer, Peacock & Co were specialist manufacturers who concentrated on locomotives, locomotive components and machine tools for locomotive construction. Within the limits of contemporary accounting knowledge, they appear to have ensured, by means of internal organisation, investment and careful cost accounting, that their goods were produced in perfect form and at as small a cost as possible. It would be interesting, if the records survived, to compare this apparently successful concern with much less successful companies and to see how their cost accounting system compared with Beyer, Peacock's. It could well be that unsuccessful companies ignored current costing knowledge to their detriment.

References

1. Charles Babbage, *On the Economy of Machinery and Manufacturers*, London 1832 p.98–99
2. Sydney Pollard, *Genesis of Modern Management. A Study of the Industrial Revolution*, London 1965 p.260
3. Manchester Museum of Science & Industry, Beyer Peacock & Company Records. First Partnership Agreement 1855.
4. Manchester Museum of Science & Industry, Beyer, Peacock & Company Records. First Minute Book January 1855. BP.M
5. Dresden Polytechnic. Inden 4 esten Jahrescursen wurde folgende wochentliche Stundenzahl ertheilt. Manchester Museum of Science & Industry, Beyer, Peacock & Company Records; Sharp Roberts Cost of Work Book
6. Public Record Office Rail 463/193 Manchester, Sheffield & Lincolnshire Railway Company – Tables showing number of miles run, consumption of Coke, total cost of each engine and general expenses in the Locomotive Department, 1849.
7. Beyer, Peacock *Quarterly Review*, Vol 1, No. 4, Oct 1927, p.14–28
8. R Peacock, On the Workshops for the Locomotive, Carriage & Wagon Department of the Manchester, Sheffield & Lincolnshire Railway *Proceedings of the Institution of Civil Engineers*, January 1851 p.22
9. Eric Roll, *An Early Experiment in Industrialisation being a History of the Firm of Boulton and Watt, 1775–1805*, London 1968
10. James Nasmyth, *An Autobiography*, edited by Samuel Smiles, London 1883 p.203

11. R Peacock op. cit.

12. *The Engineer* 12 October 1888 p.311

13. *Engineering* 4 January 1907 p.4

14. A E Musson, *James Nasmyth and the Early Growth of Mechanical Engineering*, Economic History Review, Second Series, Vol X, No. 1, 1957 p.121/127

15. Beyer, Peacock *Quarterly Review* Vol 3, No. 3, July 1929 p.65

16. *The Engineer* 25 May 1860 p.332 and Patent No. 2306, 11 October 1859

17. Beyer, Peacock *Quarterly Review* Vol 4, No. 1, January 1930 p.51

18. Manchester Museum of Science & Industry, Beyer, Peacock & Company Records. Register of Assets p.69–70. BP/BCA/1

19. Ibid p.196, 238 and 243

20. Beyer, Peacock *Quarterly Review* Vol 2, No. 1, January 1928 p.24

21. *The Engineer*, June 1856 p.333

22. Manchester Museum of Science & Industry. Beyer, Peacock & Company Records. Facsimile Letters Beyer to Robertson, 22 February 1863. BP/CBCO

23. Manchester Museum of Science & Industry. Beyer, Peacock & Company Records. Engine Order Books. General Dimension Books and Progressive Number Books BP/EOB, BP/GD, BP/PN

24. Manchester Museum of Science & Industry. Beyer, Peacock & Company Records. Wages Book 1, 12 August 1854. BP/W/1

25. Ibid Wage Book 3, 31 March 1864. BP/W/3

26. Ibid Wage Book 4, 29 March 1866. BP/W/4

27. Ibid Wage Book 11, 12 July 1890. BP/W/11

28. J F Clark, *Power on Land and Sea : A History of R & W Hawthorn Leslie*, Newcastle 1978

29. University of Glasgow, H Dübs & Company Collection UGD/9/3/1, Inventory Book 1865 p.65 Counting House

30. Manchester Museum of Science & Industry. Beyer, Peacock & Company Records. Wage analysis books survive for 1854–1869, 1884–1892 and 1918–1924. BP/W/20–BP/W/23

31. Manchester Museum of Science & Industry. Beyer, Peacock & Company Records. Cost of Work books survive from 1855. BP/CW/1–13

32. Details from Beyer, Peacock Order Books and Cost of Work Books

33. Manchester Museum of Science & Industry, Beyer, Peacock & Company Records. Agent's Illustrated Catalogue and Price List BP/P/1

34. Manchester Museum of Science & Industry, Beyer, Peacock & Company Records. Correspondence – Pihl to Beyer 18 March 1865. BP/CBCO. Engine order book No. 4 May 1866. BP/EOB/4

35. J I C Boyd, Manuscript notes. *The Engineer*, 28 June 1872. Beyer, Peacock Engine Order Book No. 11, December 1872. BP/EOB/11

36. London, India Office Library. Railway & Telegraph Department Records L/PWD/2/48. Letter from J Rendel to D J Noad, 14 January 1854

37. Manchester Museum of Science & Industry, Beyer, Peacock & Company Records. Agent's Illustrated Catalogue and Price List. BP/P/1 p.228

38. Ibid p.238

39. A E Musson, *The Growth of British Industry*, London 1978 p.145

Acknowledgements

All photographs reproduced by permission of the Manchester Museum of Science & Industry. I would like to express my thanks to the Director and staff of the Manchester Museum of Science & Industry for their help and generosity in producing the photographs for this paper.

4 Quantification and railway development before the micro-electronic revolution with special reference to the Great Western Railway and its successors

Michael Rutherford

Mathematics, Science and Engineering

The power of mathematics (rather than language and logic) as *the* fundamental mode of expression of scientific truths – particularly in conjunction with systematic experiment – was intrinsic to the philosophy of the thirteenth century English Franciscan, Roger Bacon.[1] Unfortunately he fell foul of enemies in the Church, was imprisoned for fifteen years and his works suppressed. It was Galileo Galilei, born in Florence in 1564 who set a new goal for scientific activity; a goal which has been followed ever since – that of obtaining quantitative descriptions of scientific phenomena independently of any physical explanations.[2] The application of systematic experiment to machinery was undertaken by John Smeaton (1724–92) the first man to call himself a 'civil engineer' and his experiments on wind and water mills were followed by experiments on the primitive Newcomen steam engine.[3] He was able, through detail improvements and systematic measurement, to double the output of the Newcomen engine (indeed to the practical limits of efficiency) and it continued to be built (in larger numbers than the Watt type) throughout the eighteenth and into the nineteenth century.

Measurement and the Early Railways

It had been clear from developments on the north eastern waggonways (*sic*) that a horse could pull a heavier load on a well made up cast–iron railway than on the earlier wooden type and maximum–load haulage tests are known to have been carried out on the Surrey Iron Railway in July 1805.[4] Unfortunately that company was not a financial success and the cost of traction does not seem to have been quantified. It was John Blenkinsop, viewer of the Middleton Colliery near Leeds who first anticipated that the problem of the variable nature of traction costs could be addressed by replacing renewable resources (horses and their feed – in increasing demand owing to the demands of the Napoleonic wars) by the non–renewable resources of coal and iron (in the form of locomotives). Blenkinsop prepared comparative costs of the two systems and his projected savings were proved to be correct by the success of the rack locomotives supplied by Matthew Murray's Round Foundry.

New colliery lines and renewed and extended waggonway systems from this period used horses, locomotives and both power and gravity inclines, in various combinations. This was the case with George Stephenson's earliest railways; the Hetton Colliery and the Stockton & Darlington railways. The question of the correct form of traction to use for the embryonic Liverpool & Manchester Railway was a major one from the beginning of the project and a leading civil engineer of the day, Charles Sylvester, carried out numerous tests at Hetton and Killingworth Collieries in 1824 and his results were published the following year,[5] his main conclusion being "..... I have in this report recommended the locomotive steam engine, as the most economical power, for every part of a rail–way, in which the rise is not more than 1/10 inch to a yard [ie 1 in 360]". A further report in March 1829 by James Walker and John Rastrick, based on results of enquiries made in the North East was not so positive and recommended rope haulage, mainly on the grounds of safety, but also because the locomotives that they had investigated did not appear to be able to approach the sort of speeds that the Liverpool & Manchester had in mind for their passenger services. To finally decide the matter, experiments were proposed and a stipulated list of performance characteristics were proposed for any locomotive entered for the trials, for which a prize of £500 was offered. These, the famous Rainhill Trials, began on Tuesday 6 October 1829 and were completed eight days later.[6] As is now universally known the *Rocket* of Robert Stephenson & Co, the only entrant to successfully fulfil the conditions laid down by the company, demonstrated that steam locomotive traction was the answer to the Liverpool & Manchester Railway's problem. *Rocket* showed that the multitubular boiler draughted by an exhaust blast nozzle could supply steam continuously at speed. This test locomotive was built as light as possible and with only a single pair of driving wheels, the latter detail in order to reduce to a minimum the frictional losses of the machine itself when moving a modest load at speed.

The first decade of the inter–city railway age, the 1830s, saw remarkable developments both in the steam locomotive and the railway as a complete engineering system. Much experimental work was carried out on the Liverpool & Manchester Railway; inventors and manufacturers alike being given encouragement and facilities. Success, particularly in moving passengers at speed, resulted in the ambitious plans of I K Brunel to build the Great Western Railway to the broad gauge of seven feet. The shareholders of the new Great Western Railway Company were soon divided into two main camps; that of the 'Bristol Party' – originators of the scheme, appointees of Brunel favoured the broad gauge, and the 'Liverpool Party' – rich investors from the North West who had done well from earlier schemes subscribed to the less adventurous, thrifty "narrow gauge" approach of George and Robert Stephenson, All other investors tended to side with one or other of these groups.

Matters came to a head in 1838 and the fight to save the Broad Gauge was on. The Great Western board had invited three eminent engineers to investigate and report on the railway. Robert Stephenson and James Walker (President of the Institution of Civil Engineers) both declined but Nicholas Wood accepted. It was at this point that Charles Babbage intervened in the debate and offered to carry out tests on the railway. As a shareholder and eminent man of science, he was given every assistance by the company who supplied a suitable carriage and Brunel agreed to take much of his test apparatus for future use. Babbage took the team of men, who were then working on his analytical engine, off that task for five months and embarked on the most comprehensive railway testing undertaken up until that time. He turned a passenger brake van into the first dynamometer car with purpose–built equipment from Holtzapffel & Co that recorded a number of variables onto large rolls of paper. Drawbar pull was measured as were the oscillations of the vehicle in motion.

The paper moved in proportion to the roadspeed and a special clock by Edward J Dent & Co marked the paper every half a second enabling speed to be accurately determined whenever required. Michael Faraday and Bryan Donkin advised on a number of points and Babbage's results were the most detailed and relevant yet produced. Wood reported that he was unable to find time for his own investigations and Dionysius Lardner was seconded to do his experiments for him. Lardner was offered the facility of Babbage's dynamometer car but declined and began his own measurements based on some very doubtful theory. The decisive meeting of the shareholders was held in the main dining room of the London Tavern on Wednesday 9 January 1839. Babbage savaged Lardner by demolishing his every argument and derided his methods. His own were explained in detail to such an effect that a number of northern shareholders complete with proxies, voted for the Broad Gauge, which by quite a narrow margin lived to fight another day.[7] Daniel Gooch (the Great Western Railway locomotive superintendent) took up Babbage's methods and constructed a new dynamometer car and also invented an indicator for recording the pressure in a locomotive cylinder whilst working. (Plate 4.1 and Figure 4.1) That instrument is now in the Science Museum collection.

Plate 4.1
Gooch's cylinder pressure indicator for locomotives, as preserved in the Science Museum.

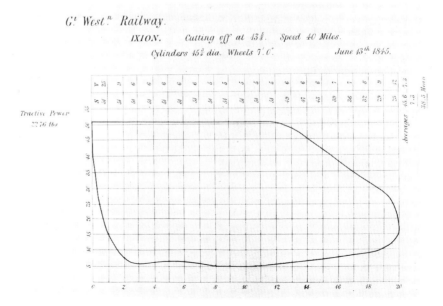

Figure 4.1
A diagram from Gooch's indicator, taken during the gauge trials.

Test results became a political issue during the gauge war of the 1840s but some years afterwards Daniel Kinnear Clark was to note: "Mr Daniel Gooch is the only experimentalist whose results are worth of implicit confidence, for he operated with the trains precisely under the conditions of ordinary service".[8]

Time and Timetables

For the first twenty years or so of steam railway operations trains ran to timetables drawn up in the manner of those prepared by stage–coach operators; a list of stops with appropriate times and a guard issued with a pre–set watch. Trains were dispatched from stations at time intervals (when on the same track) and no other form of remote signalling or control was used; only the vigilance of pointsmen, policemen (ie signalmen) and footplatemen prevented catastrophe. The speeds attained on the Broad Gauge, however, (and those on other long–distance lines in competition with each other) made necessary the development of the space–interval system or Absolute Block between trains controlled by signal boxes (or Block Posts) connected by electric telegraph and various instruments giving both visual and audible bell code information.[9] Equally important was John Saxby's patent (No 1479) of 24 June 1856 granted for a "mode of working simultaneously the points and signals of railways at junctions to prevent accidents"[10] thus interlocking the path along which the signalman directed trains and the signals indicating that path.

It was soon necessary to revise the methods of preparation of timetables and initially they were planned as distance–time graphs (often on boards using pins and coloured thread), from which, at a glance, it could be seen how extra trains or revised timings could be fitted in (Figure 4.2).

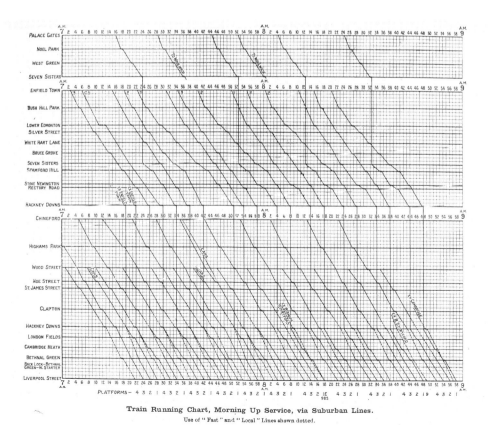

Figure 4. 2
A typical graphical timetable chart. New timetables were nearly always prepared in this way often using a peg–board and coloured threads.

Train Running Chart, Morning Up Service, via Suburban Lines.
Use of " Fast " and " Local " Lines shown dotted.

All this data was then transferred into tables of times in the official working timetables.[11] It is worth pointing out that before these new methods were introduced it was necessary for the railways to standardize on their clock time. The Great Western in particular, with its long east–west routes had to cope with considerable variations in local time between say London and Bristol (approx. 11 minutes) or Penzance (approx. 22 minutes). the Great Western standardized on London time at all its stations from November 1840, (the Bristol Corn Exchange clock still has two seperate minute hands – a survival from days of local time[12]) and by 1848 most companies including the Great Western had settled for Greenwich Mean Time (23 seconds ahead of London time). A standard was essential when planning complicated journeys using an all–company timetable such as Bradshaw, first published in 1839. It is interesting to note that a few towns still lingered on with their own local time until the Definition of Time Act of 1880 decreed that they should get into line with the rest of the nation.[13]

The Modern Era
The insistence by government on continuous *automatic* brakes (ie that automatically apply when a train is accidentally divided) on passenger trains, together with compulsory use of the Absolute Block system, following the terrible Armagh accident of 1889 brought into being new era of railway working.[14]

One of the results of these changes was the gradual introduction of much heavier express trains generally offering much higher standards of comfort with corridors throughout as well as dining and sleeping cars. Bigger and more powerful locomotives were needed for these new trains and it was soon clear that the dynamometer car was the best tool for quantifying the performance of the new types of locomotive, determining the benefits or otherwise of compounding and superheating and ascertaining the resistances of the modern trains. The Great Western (1901),[15] (Plate 4.2) North Eastern (1906), London & North Western (1908) and Lancashire & Yorkshire (1912) all built new, bogie dynamometer cars capable of absorbing high drawbar pulls.

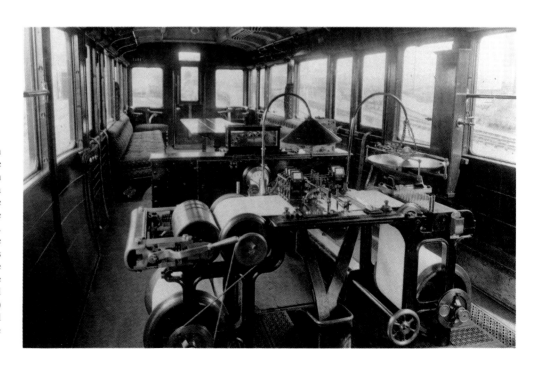

Plate 4.2
The inside of the Swindon dynamometer car of 1901. The recording paper rolls were driven by an extra wheel lowered onto a running rail as required and the paper moved at a rate proportional to the train speed. In the lower centre of the picture can be seen the massive beams that transmitted movement of the drawbar spring to both the tractive force recording pen and also to the integrating table (right) where the force was integrated with respect to time to give the total work done.

Little railway testing had been done in the latter half of the nineteenth century in Britain. Different designs of locomotives were often tried and compared on the same services and indicator diagrams were taken (many smaller, compact instruments had become available since Gooch's invention), but, in a country where some of the best coal in the world was abundantly available, there was little financial incentive for dramatic innovation. Indeed, the well–known maxim that on any train "one first–class passenger pays the coal bill" remained in vogue with the complacent until long after the need for more scientific management had become essential because of a combination of legislation, changes in labour relations and changes in economic conditions in general.

In spite of considerable work in applied thermodynamics with regard to locomotives, in the countries of continental Europe – particularly Germany, France, Belgium and Austria–Hungary, it was from the rapidly expanding railways of North America and Russia that data concerning locomotive performance was applied to the mechanics of train operating and the optimization of companies' operating costs.[16]

The first practical attempts to test steam locomotives by running trains under controlled conditions were made by Alexander Borodin in Russia in the early 1880s. It was Borodin too who made the first steps towards a stationary testing plant at Kiev around the same time.[17] Tests were conducted on a locomotive held stationary and whose driving wheels acted as belt pulleys; little power could be absorbed but useful results were obtained concerning compounding and the use of steam–jacketed cylinders. The first 'proper' locomotive test plant was built in 1890–1 at Purdue University, Lafayette, Indiana in the USA. It was built to the instructions of Prof W F M Goss as part of the engineering laboratories for the University, then under construction. A 40–ton 4–4–0 locomotive was also purchased at the same time.[18] In 1914 when he had become Dean of the College of Engineering at Illinois University, Dr Goss, together with Prof E W Schmidt (in charge of the department of railway engineering) built a very sophisticated plant, based on that of the Pennsylvania Railroad which had first been erected at the St Louis Exposition in 1904 and where a world famous series of tests were carried out on locomotive types from both Europe and the USA.[19] Illinois University also had a half share in the dynamometer car of the Illinois Central Railroad.[20] Apart from any direct benefits to locomotive engineering (and a great deal of useful research was carried out), these plants were of immense value as practical educational tools and may well be reflected in some of the quite remarkable locomotives manufactured in the later years of steam in the USA, whose mileages between repairs, general reliability and power outputs were unequalled anywhere in the world.

In Russia, Borodin's road testing ideas were taken up by G V Lomonossoff[21] who had at his disposal in Russia, a number of long straight stretches of track, some on constant gradients. It was here that locomotives could be tested at constant output and in order to improve the control of the speed at a constant value, a second, regulating locomotive was introduced which helped to start and accelerate the test train initially and added braking power. These testing methods saw the production of the 'locomotive passport' – a booklet of practical characteristics for any particular type which could then be used by the operating departments for allocating appropriate loads and speeds.

The production of such passports may well have been influenced by the accuracy of similar data that was produced for electric railways where considerably detailed services could be accurately planned before a new railway was even built.

In Britain G J Churchward of the GWR built the first modern dynamometer car in the country in 1901 (Plate 4.2) whilst still assistant to the Locomotive Superintendent, William Dean. On taking over from Dean, Churchward quickly obtained authorization for the first (and for nearly half a century, the only) stationary test plant in Britain.[22] Perhaps his new engines proved to be so successful that the plant was not really needed, at any event it was not used to any great extent in the early years.

One of Lomonossoff's pupils, Prof A Czeczott in Poland, developed the idea of the 'brake' locomotive (with the cylinders used to pump air) which could do away with all or part of the train behind the dynamometer car.[23] His method, started in 1921, was taken up by a number of other engineers, notably Nordmann and Gunther in Germany, Robson in England (on the LNER) and Chapelon in France. On the continent, electric locomotives were occasionally used, using regenerative braking and in Britain this idea developed into the Mobile Testing Plant of the LMSR.[24] All these techniques had one thing in common; they aimed to keep the locomotive under conditions of constant speed (or a series of constant speed steps). Such test trains, however, could seriously interfere with normal train operations on a busy railway; furthermore, the trailing load was produced artificially and was not a normal 'train' with characteristic resistances.

On the GWR the Controlled Road Testing system was developed which allowed trains to be worked in a normal manner, ie speed changing with gradient.[25] The controlled variable on the GW system was the locomotive steam rate (and by implication the fuel rate) which was kept at a constant value by the driver continually adjusting his cut–off (and therefore speed) in response to any deviation on a special manometer which was connected to a point below the blast pipe tip and used as an orifice meter. The road tests were preceded and complemented by tests on Swindon stationary plant which had been modernized in 1936.

Figure 4.3
Indicated tractive effort characteristics for a Great Western "Hall" class locomotive. The table shows the difference firing rates required for given outputs, depending on the quality of coal used and whether an exhaust steam injector is used or not.

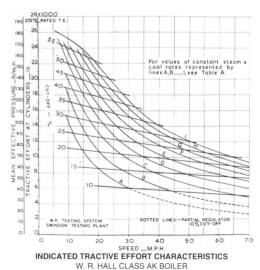

INDICATED TRACTIVE EFFORT CHARACTERISTICS
W. R. HALL CLASS AK BOILER

On the plant a locomotive could be 'tuned' and its thermodynamic characteristics established before being tested with a trailing load on the road. (Figure 4.3) An important factor was that some of the instruments in the dynamometer car were used on the stationary plant tests too; the car was located adjacent to the locomotive on test and suitable connections made. The data collected at Swindon both on the road and on the plant was analyzed and interpreted by the same team and thus a consistency in results could be expected. In the Controlled Road Testing System a speed curve was plotted for a test using thermodynamic data from the plant and known carriage resistances. The test was then carried out at the required steam rate and actual speeds plotted. (Figure 4.4)

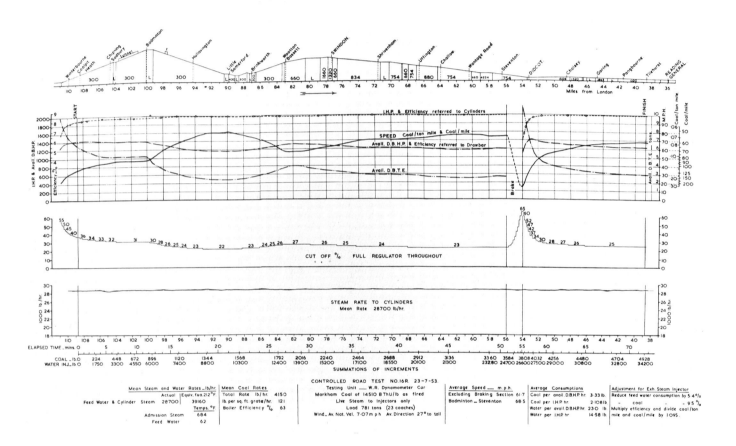

Figure 4.4
A summary graph of a Controlled Road Test using the Swindon method of constant steam and coal rates. As train speed varies with changes in gradient, the driver adjusts the cut off to keep the steam rate constant.

The speeds plotted agreed surprisingly well with those calculated and confirmed them. With a constant steam rate (or fuel rate in a diesel) the actual drawbar pull/train speed relationship is uniquely defined irrespective of gradient. The tractive force applied at the locomotive driving wheels to the whole train is a large percentage of the force produced in the cylinders and like the latter is not affected by gradient. The drawbar pull on the trailing load is in proportion to the tractive force applied to the whole train, in the ratio of the trailing mass to the gross train mass. The system has the advantage that it is operating under the Second Law of Motion which is the general equation for the motion of a train, whereas constant speed testing with brake units operates under the Third Law.[26]

One feature that developed from the system was the 'Cost of Energy Diagram' that was used by Sir Julian Tritton and J J C Paterson to illustrate their paper "The Scientific Development of Modern Locomotive Design" which was read to the British Association for the Advancement of Science at their Bristol meeting in 1955 (Figure 4.5). It could be seen at a glance from this diagram, in its modified form, the extra costs incurred in speeding up or increasing the weight of any given train using a particular type of locomotive.

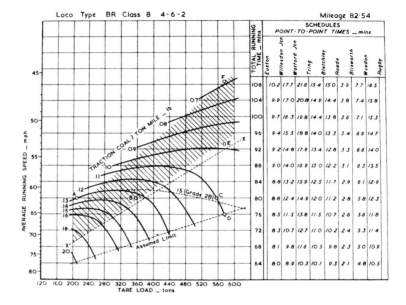

Figure 4.5
A Performance and Cost of Energy Diagram as prepared for BR class 8 4–6–2 No. 71000 Duke of Gloucester from tests on both the stationary plant at Swindon and with the dynamometer car. Results could be applied to any route whose profile and restrictions are known.

A new dynamometer car was built at Swindon in 1961 incorporating X–Y plotters and other more sophisticated equipment that took the tedium and potential sources of error from calculations and graph construction. This vehicle was very important in the determination of the characteristics of the new diesel locomotives introduced onto the Western Region and it was possible for the Swindon team under the inspired leadership of S O Ell to develop the *Passenger Train Computer* – a manual giving passing times on all routes for any weight of passenger train for different power classes of locomotive, within existing speed and other fixed limitations. The tables in this manual, which was compiled for non–engineering staff use, enabled realistic timetables to be constructed by operating staff using scientifically derived and economically sound data.[27]

From Babbage then, the Great Western could proudly show one hundred and thirty years of development by measurement and testing. Under Daniel Gooch as Locomotive Superintendent, the Company was the first to use a dynamometer car for the systematic measurement of train resistances as well as the first to develop an indicator for use on a working steam locomotive. Later, under Churchward, the first modern dynamometer car in Britain and the first stationary testing plant in Europe were constructed. Finally, by incorporating lessons learned from other parts of the world into their own practices, a methodology was developed that linked the thermodynamics of the prime-mover with the mechanics of train operating and the cost of energy to operate those trains, and was done in a way that could be applied directly to the compilation of actual timetables.

Although the Swindon testing plant no longer exists, a fine model was constructed for the Science Museum. Both the 1901 and the 1961 Dynamometer cars are in private preservation, the latter at the time of writing passed for British Rail main–line operation.

References

1. Gimpel, J (1977) *The Medieval Machine: The Industrial Revolution of the middleages*, Gollancz, London
2. Kline, M (1972) *Mathematics in Western Culture*. Pelican, London
3. Rolt, L T C and Allen, J S (1977) *The Steam Engine of Thomas Newcomen*, Moorland, Hartington
4. Tomlinson, W W (1914) *The North Eastern Railway: Its Rise and Development*
5. Sylvester, C (1825) *Report on Rail–Roads and Locomotive Engines*, Kaye, Liverpool
6. Simpson, C R H (1979) *The Rainhill Locomotive Trials*, Rainhill Trials Celebration Committee, Rainhill
7. Hyman, R A (1982) *Charles Babbage Pioneer of the Computer*, O U P, Oxford
8. Clark, D K (1955) *Railway Machinery*, Blackie & Son, Edinburgh
9. Signalling Study Group (1986) *The Signal Box*, Oxford Publishing Co
10. Westinghouse Brake & Signal Co (1956) *A Centenary of Signalling*, Westinghouse, London
11. Mallinson, J (1901) *The Compilation of a Railway Time Book*, Railway Magazine IX, pp.351–361
12. History Society for Central Bristol (1990) London Time – *Bristol fashion : Why a clock with two minute hands?* Yesterday Transport Digest No. 28, pp.23–4
13. Malin, S and Stott, C (1984) *The Greenwich Meridian*, Ordnance Survey, Southampton
14. Rolt, L T C (1976, 3rd ed) *Red For Danger*, David & Charles, Newton Abbot
15. Anon (1923) *Dynamometer Car Used on the Great Western Railway*, Railway Engineer *44*, pp.466–472
16. Henderson, G R (1906) *The Cost of Locomotive Operation*, Railway Gazette, London
17. Carling, D R (1972) *Locomotive Testing Stations (Pts I & II)*, Transactions of the Newcomen Society, *XLV*
18. Goss, W F M (1909) *Locomotive Performance*, Wiley & Son, New York
19. Pennsylvania Railroad Co (1905), *Locomotive Tests and Exhibits*, Philadelphia
20. Tuthill, J K (1947) *The Railroad Dynamometer Car of the University of Illinois and the Illinois Central Railroad*. University of Illinois Bulletin *45* No. 11
21. Lomonossoff, G V (1926) *Lokomotiv–Versuche in Russland*, VDI–Verlag, Berlin
22. Anon (1905) *Locomotive Testing Plant at Swindon*, Engineer *100*
23. Czeczott, A (1931) *A description of the method of carrying out locomotive tests on the Polish State Railways*, Bulletin of the International Railway Congress Association XIII No. 7
24. Andrews, H I (1948) *The Mobile Locomotive Testing Plant of the London, Midland and Scottish Railway*, Proc. I Mech E, *158*
25. Ell, S O (1953) *Developments in Locomotive Testing*, Journal of the Institution of Locomotive Engineers *43*, Part 1 (Paper 527)
26. Ell, S O (1958) *The Mechanics of the Train in the Service of Railway Operation*, Journal I Loco E *48*, Part 5 (Paper 528)
27. Ell, S O (c.1964) *Passenger Train Computer – Western Region* – Second Edition, BRB, Swindon

5 Railway electrification in London and its social effects

Michael Robbins

'Railway electrification' is an ambiguous term. To electrify a railway would normally be expected to mean equipping an existing line, worked by steam traction, so that haulage by means of electric motors, continuously fed with current from an outside source, can be employed. But to adopt this definition would rule out newly-constructed railways intended from the start to be electrically worked. This would restrict the subject matter unduly by importing an unnecessary distinction and make useful analysis of results almost impossible. Certain railways were from the start designed and constructed solely for electric traction. Indeed, the low–level 'tube' railways with crossovers and junctions could not be operated with any other form of motive power; cable traction had been considered at the outset for the City & South London Railway and, wisely, rejected. 'Railway electrification' must be understood as the provision of railways worked by electrical power.

But why should this provision have had any social effect at all? To substitute one form of railway motive power for another might be regarded as an affair of internal significance only, introduced for management reasons of efficiency or economy, with some important but incidental effects on the environment when a cleaner and quieter method of moving trains along railway lines was adopted. These management reasons were of course present; but the economies were not sufficient to pay the interest on the substantial capital outlay involved. To put it shortly and to state the norm from which individual cases here and there diverged: outlay on electrification of existing railways did not enable existing traffics to be moved more cheaply, when interest on the new capital investment was taken into account; but it did provide potential capacity to move much larger traffics, which could not have been moved at all under previous conditions of motive power and operation. Electrification was almost invariably undertaken when large new traffics could be foreseen.

There were, it is true, a few cases (though none in London) where an alternative to steam traction had to be found because the conditions of operation within tunnels had come to be considered unacceptable. This seems to have happened first in Britain on the Quayside branch at Newcastle, on the North Eastern Railway, in 1905. In the United States there were several examples, including the earliest, through the city of Baltimore, 1895; the Cascade mountain section of the Great Northern Railway, 1909; the Hoosac tunnel on the Boston & Maine RR, 1911; and the approaches to the New York City terminals of the New York Central, New Haven, and Pennsylvania railroads, required by an act of the state of New York (1903) to be carried out by 1908. The LNER Woodhead tunnel electrification, approved in 1936 and completed in 1954, was similar in character to these; but there was nothing of the sort in the London area.

Electrification by itself, however, if it was not accompanied by other improvements, was far from a complete solution. Change in motive power alone was not going to provide capacity for a greatly increased volume of traffic. Many other things had to be done to enable more trains to be moved along the lines and turned at the terminals: improved signalling (often using electrical systems in place of mechanical), more track loops and connections, new and better–sited depots for rolling stock, and improved track layouts at terminals and junctions. All electrifications were accompanied by such improvements, so that it is virtually impossible to distinguish between the effects of the new motive power and the effects of other improvements, which were often very substantial. Added to this, fares and season–ticket rates were often adjusted at the time of electrification to make them more attractive; and these changes would have led to some increase in travel anyway.

Enthusiasts for the retention of steam traction often claimed that the expansion of traffic that was achieved could all have been obtained by the track and signalling improvements alone. The Great Eastern Railway, though it took powers to electrify its suburban lines in 1903, was particularly sceptical about the advantages of such large investment, and it put on some striking demonstrations of the still unrealised potential of steam working. First, in 1903, it produced the 'Decapod' locomotive,which managed to accelerate a 335–ton train from start to 30 mph in just under 30 seconds, but which would have required all the bridges on the lines it used to be rebuilt to sustain its weight. The railway did more impressively in 1920. Careful stop–watch observations were made of the use of tracks and signals, engine sidings with water–columns, and passenger circulating areas – a case of operational research twenty years before that name was invented. Modifications based on this investigation enabled the railway to run on one track up the bank from Liverpool Street to Bethnal Green 24 trains an hour (one every 2½ minutes), each of 16 coaches having 48 seats, loading up to 1200 passengers, hauled by small and mostly ancient steam locomotives. No main–line electric service had yet beaten that. Observers from other railways and other countries went to Liverpool Street to witness this phenomenon, and they were wont to say, like the first European traveller to see a giraffe, that they didn't believe it.

But the Great Eastern's was not the way ahead. It demonstrated the utmost limit to which an obsolescent technology could be driven. Electric railway technology was developing only slowly, but it held the potential for huge expansion. The Underground railways, the Metropolitan under R H Selbie, the London, Brighton & South Coast, and the London & South Western and the Southern under Sir Herbert Walker showed what must be. They built their new electric railways or electrified their old ones with their eyes on the creation of new traffics, not merely on the more efficient handling of existing ones. They were calculating on expansion of their basic traffic, the journey to and from work, from new settlement in and around existing suburbs and from new housing all down their lines. They also counted, and this was important, on creating new traffic to occupy seats in their trains between the working peaks and in the evenings by offering attractive services (and often cheap fares) to and from town for other members of the breadwinner's family to use. So naturally the first phase of railway electrification in London (apart from the Brighton's South London line and the North London, which were designed to counter competition from electric tramways) provided electric railways to higher-income areas like Hampstead and Highgate, Harrow, Ealing, Richmond and Wimbledon from where housewives and retired people with sufficient incomes might reasonably be expected to want to travel to Town for occasional shopping or entertainment or for other social reasons. This would not apply to Tottenham or Walthamstow or Lewisham in anything like the same degree, if indeed it did so at all. So the electrified railways in the earlier phase showed a marked bias of distribution to the north–western, western and south–western suburbs of London, where middle–class rather than working–class suburbs had already been established. Later on, other considerations began to apply, and government support, first by guarantee of interest and after 1948 by capital contributions, had to be secured for electrifications through districts where traffic outside the peaks was likely to be much thinner.

The word 'Metro–land' is evocative of the early phase. The name, first coined in 1915 for the Metropolitan Railway's publicity, was the perfect label for this aspect of the social process. All trains north of Harrow–on–the–Hill were still steam–hauled; but the services that made Metro–land popular, Pullman cars and all, could not have been worked in and out of London except by electricity. With Metro–land must also be mentioned the name of its Poet Laureate, Sir John Betjeman. (I include some lines of his with particular pleasure because they come from one of three poems which he acknowledged to have been written at my encouragement.) This poem is called *The Metropolitan Railway: Baker Street Station Buffet*. It begins:

> "Early Electric! With what radiant hope ..."

and two verses of it run:

> "Smoothly from Harrow, passing Preston Road,
>   They saw the last green fields and misty sky,
> At Neasden watched a workmens' train unload,
>   And, with the morning villas sliding by,
> They felt so sure on their electric trip
> That Youth and Progress were in partnership.
>
> And all that day in murky London Wall
>   The thought of Ruislip kept him warm inside;
> At Farringdon that lunch hour at a stall
>   He bought a dozen plants of London Pride;
> While she, in arc–lit Oxford Street adrift,
> Soared through the sales by safe hydraulic lift."

Quoted from John Betjeman, *A few late Chrysanthemums* (1954), pp. 38-9, by permission of John Murray (Publishers) Ltd.

It must have been a January day. What an eye and ear for Edwardian detail! What a poet's vision of Middlesex and London!

The mention of London Wall leads to an important point: the effect on the inner parts of London. The underground railways came quickly to be regarded as convenient and acceptable modes of travel within central London by virtually every kind of people. Permanent Secretaries travelled to Whitehall by the District (probably in the first class), though it does not seem that Bertie Wooster is recorded as ever going by tube – still, he presumably had to take an electric train when he made surreptitious visits to Valley Fields (*sc* West Dulwich). The effect of the tubes, as the effect of the Metropolitan and District railways had been in the 1860s and 1870s, was to postpone for another generation and more the arrival of an intolerable state of congestion on the streets.

A similar effect was the continued and often growing strength of Central London shopping and entertainment. These activities had developed westwards from the Strand area during the 19th century, as Shaftesbury Avenue and Charing Cross Road of the 1880s, with the earlier New Oxford Street, brought salubrity and improvement to what had been slummy, tumbledown areas. As the suburbs expanded at ever–increasing distances from Town, Oxford Street and Theatreland still held their own, very largely because of easy transport to and from them by rail. The out–of–town shopping centre, confidently prophesied, on the basis of American experience, to steal the retail trade from the central West End, has been slow to develop round London. The Whitgift Centre at Croydon and Brent Cross are there, certainly, with shops offering a far wider selection of goods than their predecessors in suburban shopping parades. Many of their customers travel by electric train; but Oxford Street and Knightsbridge have continued to flourish.

Plate 5.1
Underground Poster, 1907, artist
unknown.
(*London Transport Museum*)

But the principal impact of railway electrification was to be felt in the suburbs. London had indeed had considerable suburbs based on horse–drawn road transport before there were any railways at all: Peckham, Clapham, Hammersmith, and Highgate were plainly recognisable suburbs before railways reached them. But outside that kind of radius, say at most forty minutes' horse–bus ride, the steam railway created a girdle of new suburban settlement, changing the character of old towns and villages like Enfield, Harrow, Kingston, Croydon and Bromley and filling in some (though by no means all) of the intervening spaces, either with new, deliberately planned layouts like Surbiton, parts of Willesden Green, and Bush Hill Park at Edmonton, or with the kind of piecemeal development in small parcels that was more usual. These were unevenly distributed, with a bias to the south and east of London, because the railways on those sides, with less long–distance traffic and not much freight, were quicker to look for local passengers. So there was in these districts a pattern of 'railway suburbs' that looked on the Ordnance maps like a succession of beads on a string, the centre of each bead–like blob being a railway station.

'Suburbs' means here those districts linked to London by more or less continuous building, a considerable proportion of whose earning inhabitants perform their daily work outside the district in which they reside (not necessarily in the centre of London). So the facility of transport is inherent in the nature of suburbs: not that transport by itself produces suburbs, but the opposite is true: no transport, no suburb. And it may be added: more transport, more suburbs. So, assuming a future with assured industrial and economic prospects and a rise in population, the railway managements who electrified their London lines for growth prospects are seen to have been right. The change, it is true, was not one of kind but one of degree. But the two things, electrification and the accompanying improvements to the physical layout of the systems, between them unlocked a Pandora's box of new passenger–carrying capacity. They gave the resulting to–and–fro movement so strong a boost that the results seemed almost of a new kind altogether.

Two figures are enough to show the scale and impact of this. Between 1925 and 1934 gross passenger takings on the Southern's Hayes branch (three stations) increased almost twelvefold. Between 1927 and 1937 the number of season tickets issued at New Malden and Surbiton, already well developed in the steam age and by eleven years of electrification, increased two and a half times. New Malden and Surbiton and all the old suburban centres had to be transformed, with new shops, schools, churches, cinemas and local government; residents' associations came too, to stimulate local government and often to combat it. What was more, the new trains could make more stops on the way to Town and still cut the journey time (it was not their top speed that counted but the performance in acceleration and braking). So new stations were opened, each of them becoming the central point of a new community. On the group of electric lines served from Waterloo, nine new stations were opened between 1916 and 1936, nearly all of them with contributions of land or money put up by developers of housing estates; and there were four more new stations on the Chessington branch of 1938–9. The new Wimbledon and Sutton line of 1929–30 had six new stations. On the rest of the Southern, and on all electrically–worked London railways to some extent, more stations were opened. One incidental result was a considerable expansion in steam–worked freight services, first to carry building materials for the construction of the new settlements and then to keep them supplied with coal for their domestic grates. But electric traction played no part in that movement.

The Underground and the Southern were the leaders. The main lines east and north of London had to wait until after the war of 1939–45 for their electrifications – even the London, Tilbury & Southend, which should have been electrified as part of the bargain whereby the Midland Railway absorbed the LT&S company in 1912. These post–war electrifications brought frequent services to the first generation of new Towns – Stevenage, Hemel Hempstead, Harlow and Basildon (Crawley already had them) – which helped to resettle Londoners as residents of satellites.

What social implications of this vastly increased mobility can be perceived? At the time and often since, the commentators have been generally contemptuous. An Oxford intellectual of the 1930s, G D H Cole, wrote: "There are an astonishing number of suburbs round London that are very like this suburb of mine [that he had just been describing] and I doubt if, in the whole history of mankind, there has ever been a type of place so lacking in the spirit of community or democracy or in any sort of unity save that of mere physical juxtaposition". In the whole history of mankind! This passage was quoted, apparently with approval, in the *Greater London Plan 1944*. Intellectual persons dwelling in Hampstead, the product of an earlier suburban movement, could see nothing likely to lead towards their idea of the good life in the Avenues, Gardens and Closes of Ruislip in Middlesex or Hayes in Kent. These people did not like semi–detached houses, even though these had begun acceptably enough in St John's Wood. They did not care for the look of the places, if they looked at them at all, so they thought that life there must be drab and worthless: the architectural fallacy. And they duly deplored, being right–minded people, the lack of any overall scheme of planning.

The growth of 20th–century suburbs derived its character from many sources and was subject to many influences. Growing population and sharper perceptions of the standards fitting for the accommodation of human beings would in any case have required large additions to the total stock of houses, and places of employment too, and facilities for recreation. When settlements are established on land not previously built on and with no existing nucleus of settlement, broadly one of two contrasting arrangements has to be adopted: planned or unplanned – 'planned' meaning not only physically planned but planned with a view to a particular kind of community life. The founders of the earliest settlements in New England set up a framework of community life under strict control, from religion to economics and conduct and dress, because they could conceive no other way of creating the sort of community they wanted. (Later, some of their people went away and kept on pushing farther and farther west to escape from the authoritarian regime and indeed from any authority at all.) The creators of the Hampstead Garden Suburb and the garden cities at Letchworth and Welwyn provided carefully, indeed paternalistically, for communal activity. Letchworth and Welwyn were situated on steam railways, Hampstead (garden 'suburb', not 'city') on an electric tube. Ebenezer Howard, in his influential book of 1898 best known as *Garden Cities of Tomorrow*, paid some attention to transport, showing a formal pattern of railway lines in his ideal schemes; the New Town planners of the post–1945 period were equally vague about the transport elements of their schemes.

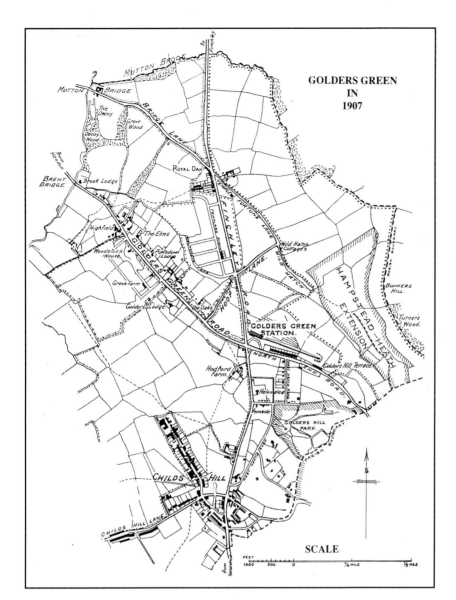

GOLDERS GREEN IN 1907

Fig 5.1
Golders Green in 1907, the year
the Underground electric railway
was opened.

SCALE

Plate 5.2
Golders Green crossroads: the
station site in 1904.
(London Transport Museum)

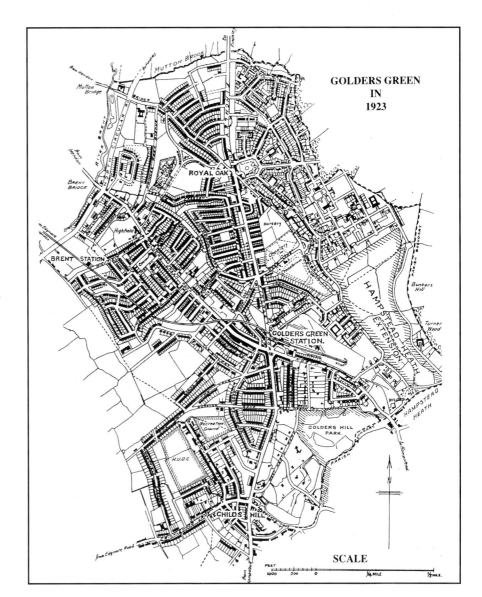

Fig 5.2
Development of Golders Green to 1923.
(from F. Howkins, The Story of Golders Green and its Remarkable Development, Ernest Owers Ltd, Golders Green, 1923)

Plate 5.3
Golders Green crossroads, about 1920.
(from a postcard: London Transport Museum)

The other kind of development – run up the houses and the workplaces, and let the people who come there make their own arrangements – was characteristic of most of the 19th–century industrial expansions. Such planned communities as there were – the first settlement at Middlesbrough, Saltaire, Bournville, Port Sunlight – were so rare as to be conspicuous exceptions. On the whole the London suburbs were unplanned. It was up to the people who went to live in them whether they would live their lives in a fragmented, individualistic way or get themselves organized into groups.

The particular directions that the development of London suburbs followed were very largely determined by the facility of personal transport. Here the electrified railway was overwhelmingly important. Road transport could meet no more than a fraction of the demand; only the railway could handle the huge movements. So the railway pattern was dominant. With trifling exceptions (the North London line from Broad Street to Richmond, the East London, the South London and the funny little Wimbledon – West Croydon line), the railways carried people to and from London, or intermediately, along generally radial lines. So to many people, perhaps the majority in the newer suburbs, their home could become just a place to sleep in, from which the earners emerged to take a more or less convenient journey to somewhere else where they worked. There may not have been much for the earner's wife to interest herself in. Add to this that they were typically migrants from another part of London or from somewhere else altogether and did not expect to stay where they were for very long; and there were the ingredients for a society consisting of a rootless, floating population. For such temporary residents, local ties apart from shops and doctor and school, and perhaps church, might be very slight. Many suburbans did not know, or did not care, what local authority area they lived in; Harrow, where the borough council was, meant very little to people with an address in Stanmore. Central London, or the firms for which they worked, could stand for something much more important to them than their local community.

For all of that, easy access and mobility may be blamed. But was the whole process a social disaster? It is possible, and surely right, to take a more reflective view. Electric railways enabled a beneficial social transformation to take place, with improvement of life, a move away from overcrowding to cleaner air, less cramped schools, a garden or an allotment. This was not only for the middle classes, as is sometimes asserted: the London County Council's rehousing estates at White City, Dagenham/Becontree, Watling (Burnt Oak), St Helier and (in part) Downham depended on electric rail transport. Indeed, it may be argued not that electrification led to undesirable suburbs but that there was not enough of it soon enough. Unusually for London, in the district of North Ilford round Eastern Avenue housing had gone far in advance of travel facilities, and the inhabitants formed an active pressure group in 1934 to get an electric railway of some kind. Places without electric trains clamoured for them. Passengers on the Tilbury line and the Great Eastern and Great Northern lines demanded it; weary travellers on the High Barnet branch anxiously crossed off the days on their calendars, longing for the promised electrics to come. Delay in the electrification of the local railway meant postponement of social improvement. It would have been better for London if its railways had carried through the process of electrification much sooner.

The usual gloomy view of suburban life expressed by writers in the 1930s and later needs a corrective; and fortunately evidence is conveniently available. This is an account of the community at Stoneleigh, an area developed without overall plan by various builders. There was no existing nucleus, apart from a station opened by the Southern Railway in 1932 between Worcester Park and Ewell. The story is chronicled in sufficient detail in Alan Jackson's admirable book *Semi–Detached London* (Allen & Unwin, 1973), pp.272–90. Physically, this suburb was not satisfactory: the developers missed their chance of making it so by failing to use its undulating site and the surviving woodland with any imagination; and the very railway that brought it into being was a barrier dividing the place into two portions with only two crossings in a mile and a half. But community activity was very lively – a strong residents' association (whose candidates carried all three wards in the borough elections of 1938), a choral society and an orchestra, and all manner of clubs, including ones for cycling, tennis and keeping fit. If voluntary associations are a good index of social responsibility, that suburb should rank high. There is plenty of evidence that Stoneleigh was typical rather than unusual in this respect.

But that was the kind of thing that the intellectuals of the 1930s failed to notice. The mobility given by the electric train enabled people to choose: they could be socially active, as many were, in their home districts; or they could enjoy privacy in a way that they could not have done in crowded areas. A much greater measure of freedom for people to choose how they might live was the gift that the electric railway conferred.

One does not usually look to advertising handouts for reliable prophecies about long–term future developments, nor do they often risk making them. But when the Hampstead tube was opened in 1907, the railway's publicity proclaimed that its passengers would "enter into possession of a complete system of underground railway transit which it is believed will not only help to solve the pressing problems of street traffic but will introduce wide–ranging changes in the distribution of population, the location of shopping centres and the travel habits of the people". (Use of the word 'transit' betrayed the transatlantic origins of the moving spirits in the undertaking.) About street congestion they were right, though not for long; about shopping centres, only partly right; but as to the travel habits of the people they were absolutely right. In 1901 each inhabitant of the Greater London area had on average taken 177 journeys by rail, bus and tram transport. In 1921 the number had risen to 364; in 1938/9 to 443; in 1948, the peak year for public transport, to 524.

Travel forms such a large part of urban and suburban life that it is not far–fetched to say that electric railways wrought a revolution in London. If it had not happened, the place would have become unworkable in the Edwardian decade. Now, in the nineties, it needs to be made workable and endurable again; and the key to its regeneration will again be transport.

6 The fifteen inch gauge steam locomotives of Bassett-Lowke

David Mosley

The fifteen inch gauge steam locomotives built by the renowned model engineering firm of Bassett–Lowke of Northampton in the early years of this century bring together a number of little known but nonetheless fascinating strands in the history of small gauge railways.

By no means the first to use the fifteen–inch gauge as a standard, Bassett–Lowke drew together the experimental work of the Heywood railways with the commercial developments made by the Cagney brothers in the United States. Locomotives like *Little Giant* bridged the gap between the narrowest practical gauge and the world of model engineering.

At the turn of the century the railway, in all its forms, was seen as the panacea for all transport problems. The main–line railway was the dominant form of land–transport, narrow gauge lines penetrated difficult and remote areas whilst experimental engineers sought the narrowest gauge which would be both technically feasible and economically viable. One such engineer was Arthur, later Sir Arthur, Heywood of Duffield Bank in Derbyshire; an archetypal Victorian gentleman engineer. Heywood was concerned "to put into practice the views I had formed in regard to the possibility of advantageously superseding horse traction, in cases where a traffic, though heavy, was wholly insufficient to justify a more costly railway".[1]

His ideas were to cover country estates, military installations, public institutions and small industries where the traffic between two fixed points would be no more than ten thousand tons per year. By 1874 Heywood had determined that the fifteen inch gauge was "the smallest width possessing the necessary stability for practical use"[2] and he began construction of a demonstration line at his home at Duffield Bank. Completed by 1881 the Duffield Bank Railway, built on a spectacular hillside, was about half a mile long and included severe gradients, several tunnels and a prefabricated viaduct over 90 feet long and 20 feet high as well as the usual stations, sidings and signals. In building the line Heywood had used 'Effie', an 0–4–0T built in his own works at Duffield Bank, but the 'standard' Heywood locomotive appeared with the opening of the line. 'Ella' was an 0–6–0T, pure narrow gauge with no concession to scale and built to the maximum dimensions allowed by the gauge.

The Duffield Bank Railway's public opening coincided with the 1881 Royal Agricultural Show held at Derby and visitors to the Show were able to inspect the line. Seemingly, agricultural interests were unimpressed by the possibilities of the fifteen inch gauge and no orders were forthcoming. The line thus reverted to being an engineering experiment, a source of enjoyment for the Heywood family and the villagers of Duffield and an interesting technical day out for visitors to the works of the Midland Railway, five miles away at Derby. A second public exhibition in 1894 did produce an order for a line at Eaton Hall, the Duke of Westminster's seat near Chester. This proved to be the ultimate, and only, manifestation of a Heywood railway in action and in the years up to the First World War proved an interesting link between the Heywood and Bassett–Lowke schools of thought in providing a venue where two of the latter's locomotives were tested.

The Heywood lines were not a commercial success. Duffield Bank closed on Sir Arthur's death in 1916, the Eaton Hall Railway lingered on in reduced circumstances until 1947. Heywood's work did prove, however, that the fifteen inch gauge was a safe passenger carrier and so influenced others that it became a miniature standard. Heywood was concerned with the use of the fifteen inch gauge to solve transport problems; the pioneering work in the use of the gauge in the business of pleasure came from across the Atlantic. In the United States short passenger carrying lines operated for pleasure in amusement parks and at exhibitions. Amongst the principal promoters of railways of this sort were the four brothers Cagney trading as the Miniature Railroad Company of Broadway, New York. The Cagneys used locomotives of $12\frac{5}{8}$, 15, 18 and 22 inch gauge but they concentrated on a single prototype, the legendary flyer 4–4–0 No. 999 of the New York Central & Hudson River Railroad. In 1901 Cagney locomotives appeared in Britain and a most successful line was operated at the Glasgow International Exposition.

Plate 6.1
The first Cagney locomotive in the country is admired by visitors to the Glasgow International Exhibition of 1901. The functional lines of the locomotive are apparent.
(National Railway Museum)

In 1903 a more permanent line was constructed by Charles Bartholomew in grounds of his home, Blakesley Hall near Towcester, using at least one Cagney 15 inch gauge 4–4–0. It is at this point that W J Bassett–Lowke enters the story. Already making his way in the model engineering world and already setting standards for scale realism the Cagney locomotives must have seemed to him a crude construction which could surely be bettered. Although a self–styled 'internationalist in thought' Bassett–Lowke apparently considered that British manufacture could do better and the 15 inch gauge represented a potential business opportunity.

Wenman Joseph Bassett–Lowke was born in Northampton in 1877. His father ran a small engineering business and it was expected that the young Bassett–Lowke would follow in his father's footsteps. This was the case for a short while and at one time he was apprenticed to the electrical firm of Crompton–Parkinson at Colchester. Model engineering was Bassett–Lowke's first love, however, and he began to develop a small business. This showed him that although there were many interested model engineers their sources of supply were very limited. Bassett–Lowke therefore set out to supply components; he began to publish catalogues and to import complete model locomotives from well–established firms on the Continent such as Bing and Carette. All the time, in the sphere of railway modelling, his concern was to establish realism.

At the turn of the century, Bassett–Lowke met Henry Greenly. Greenly was an enthusiastic railway modeller who had studied engineering and architecture at the Regent Street Polytechnic before joining the drawing office of the Metropolitan Railway in 1897. He subsequently left this post to join the new Percival Marshall magazine 'Model Engineer' and in 1904 he wrote *The Model Locomotive*. Greenly was soon designing models for Bassett–Lowke but it was as a designer of 15 inch gauge steam locomotives that he was to prove his true worth. In 1904 Bassett–Lowke added another section to his expanding business with the formation of 'The Miniature Railways of Great Britain Ltd'. Backed by a number of Northampton businessmen and with Henry Greenly as engineer the aim of the company was not merely to supply miniature railway equipment but also to operate complete railways. The first venture, a $10^{1}/_{4}$ inch gauge line at Northampton at Easter 1905 proved the possibilities for the company.

Fifteen inch gauge was chosen as the standard to which Miniature Railways of Great Britain should work but in the true Bassett–Lowke spirit of realism the locomotives were to be quarter–scale models rather than exploiting the full potential of the gauge in Heywood fashion. It was felt that a recognisable diminutive would have considerable appeal to potential passengers. To build the proposed locomotives a Large Scale Model Shop was added to the Bassett–Lowke workshops and a staff of five was employed. The end product was the "rolling–out", on 26 April 1905, of Greenly's first 15 inch gauge locomotive *Little Giant*. A quarter scale 4–4–2, the freelance design compared in beauty of form with full size North Eastern and Great Central Railways' locomotives of the time and in construction and finish was a much more sophisticated product than the Cagneys. In production Greenly had followed American practice by use of cast steel for such components as wheels, crossheads, connecting rods and frame stretchers, the short fixed wheel base of the locomotive allowed for the negotiation of sharp curves and the main frames were of $^{1}/_{4}$ inch steel plate cut by hand and shaped by hand–filing – a job reckoned to be a month's hard labour for one man! The boiler, built at the works of Bassett–Lowke senior, was 3' 5" long and 1' 3" wide carrying 37 brass tubes, original working pressure was 110psi although this was subsequently raised by 10psi. Stephenson's valve gear was used and Greenly's own design of steam brake was fitted. A six wheeled tender carried 35 gallons of water and $\frac{1}{2}$cwt of coke. (For full details see Appendix 1)

Plate 6.2
In its original form and resplendent in maroon livery Little Giant is seen at Blackpool in 1905.
(National Railway Museum)

Little Giant was destined for Miniature Railways of Great Britain's first 15 inch gauge venture, a quarter mile circuit of track on Blackpool's South Shore. On the way from Northampton to Blackpool the opportunity was taken to 'road–test' the new locomotive on the Duke of Westminster's line at Eaton Hall. Here, under the eyes of some distinguished enthusiasts, *Little Giant* proved itself to be both fleet and powerful. A maximum load of 12 tons was hauled and with lighter loads speeds of over 20 mph could be sustained on favourable sections of the line. Operations at Blackpool began on Whit Monday 1905 and *Little Giant* soon repaid the company's commercial faith by hauling over 9000 passengers in the first week. The success of the operation brings up a parallel between the experiences of Miniature Railways of Great Britain and Sir Arthur Heywood; despite the undoubted engineering success no flood of orders was forthcoming and no–one appeared enthusiastic to outlay something over £300 for an ex–works *Little Giant*.

In 1907 Miniature Railways of Great Britain opened a 10¼ inch gauge line at Sutton Park, Sutton Coldfield. By 1908 this had become 15 inch gauge and the second of the *Little Giant* type "Atlantics", named *Mighty Atom*, was provided. Two small "Atlantics" constituted a class and the *Little Giants* are usually referred to as Class 10. The next year Miniature Railways of Great Britain provided a railway for the International Exposition at Nancy, the first of their continental ventures.

The despatch of the locomotive No. 12 *Entente Cordiale* was recorded in the new Bassett–Lowke house magazine *Model Railways and Locomotives*,

> "Several improvements are to be effected in the design from the experience at Sutton Park (near Birmingham) and South Shore, Blackpool. A bogie tender is to be used ..... this is rendered necessary by the greater water capacity required ..... and to allow of sharper curves being negotiated. The water capacity of the new tender will be 50 gallons. As ample heating surface was available in previous designs, the tubes in this locomotive will be slightly increased to render steam–raising somewhat easier. An outside trailing axle box .... is also contemplated".[3]

This last modification did not appear in fact until the larger Class 20 engines two years later.

Plate 6.3
Class 10 "Atlantic" No 15 Red Dragon at the White City in 1909. The operation is typical of Miniature Railways of Great Britain, specifically supplied locomotive, ornate carriages and overstated staff uniforms.
(John Harrison/NRM collection)

Such was the success of the line at Nancy that a second locomotive was despatched. *Ville de Nancy* was in fact *Mighty Atom* renamed and reliveried and this incident was the start of a Bassett–Lowke trait, the cavalier renumbering and naming of locomotives upon their transfer to other lines. In continuation of this trait engine No. 14 was no other than *Little Giant*, renamed *Little Elephant* in 1910 on transferral to the line at Halifax Zoo. Engines No 15 and No 16, *Red Dragon* and *Green Dragon*, both built with boilers slightly larger than their predecessors, were intended for the White City Imperial International Exhibition of 1909. Only No 15 was used, No 16 undoubtedly metamorphosing into one of the three locomotives which Miniature Railways of Great Britain provided for the

Brussels Exhibition of 1910. Other continental lines were subsequently run at Roubaix, Cologne and Breslau and a further new Class 10 locomotive was joined by *Entente Cordiale* in their operation. No 18 *George the Fifth* was built in 1911 for the Llewellyn Miniature Railway at Southport whilst Class 10 was completed in 1912 by No 19 *Hungaria* which operated first at Geneva and later in Budapest. [A detailed summary of the various locations of the Bassett–Lowke steam locomotives is given in Appendix 2]

1911 saw the last venture undertaken by Miniature Railways of Great Britain. This was the Rhyl Miniature Railway and following its completion the functions of the company were taken over by Bassett–Lowke's next venture, Narrow Gauge Railways Ltd. In the same year three new designs of 15 inch gauge locomotives appeared on the drawing board of Henry Greenly; the years up to the First World War saw the Northampton Large Model Shop turn these into reality.

The first of these designs was an *"Improved Little Giant"* known as Class 20. Three of these were built: they had larger boilers than Class 10 locomotives, larger cylinders with forced lubrication and a grid superheater. In outward appearance they differed from Class 10, having outside axleboxes on the trailing wheels and a single flat–topped splasher covering both driving wheels. The price of an ex–works Class 20 was £320, the price actually having dropped since the appearance of *Little Giant* in 1905! The first Class 20 went, in 1912, to King Rama VI of Siam thus reinforcing one of the 15 inch gauge's interesting coincidences, the same monarch having a few years earlier taken delivery of a nickel–plated Cagney 4–4–0. The other two Class 20s stayed at home. In 1912 No 21 *Prince of Wales* went to Southport whilst in 1916 No 22 *Prince Edward of Wales* opened Narrow Gauge Railways final venture at Fairbourne in Merionethshire.

The first of the Class 30 "Atlantics" appeared in December 1912 and may well have been a speculative venture as it was reported that "the new engine, not being immediately required for the company's (Narrow Gauge Railways') work, has been purchased by Sir Robert Walker of Sand Hutton, York".[4] To be named *Synolda* the locomotive was "over 30 per cent more powerful than the previous engines".[5] It had 19 inch driving wheels, a 55 gallon tender and a wide firebox with the trailing wheels having outside radial axleboxes. *Synolda* and her two sisters were larger engines than the Class 10s and 20s being built to a scale of 3¼ inches to the foot rather than 3 inches to the foot as with their predecessors. No 31 *Sanspareil*, built in 1913 was intended for service at Geneva but made her debut in Oslo in 1914. No 32 *Count Louis* was not completed until 1923 from parts prepared in 1914.

The final Bassett–Lowke 15 inch gauge locomotive to be built was a "Pacific". Mr J.E.P. Howey, later to achieve fame as the creator of the Romney, Hythe & Dymchurch Railway, required a locomotive to run on his Staughton Manor Railway in Huntingdonshire; the Bassett–Lowke/Greenly answer was the Class 60 4–6–2 *John Anthony*. Completed in January 1914 the Class 60 appeared in the Bassett–Lowke catalogue as "Gigantic" – a singular lapse in taste perhaps brought on by contemporary maritime practice – and was a much enlarged Class 30 (see Appendix 1). As the Staughton Manor line was a modest affair, Howey looked for a larger line to test his puissant "Pacific".

Plate 6.4
"The number of Pacifics has doubled overnight" exclaimed the Railway Magazine on the appearance of Mr Howey's Class 60. The locomotive, soon to be named *John Anthony*, is seen as Staughton Manor in the Spring of 1914.
(*National Railway Museum*)

A second series of trials thus came to be held at Eaton Hall in July 1914. *John Anthony* was able to move a load of 16 tons at 13 mph on the level and was able to sustain 24 mph with 5 tons. "For a speed test the wagons were detached and a run made with the brake van alone. On this journey a top speed of 32.4 mph was reached on the level. A still higher speed of no less than 34.6 mph was attained by running the engine light and this proved truly a thrilling experience for the driver. It was not deemed advisable to 'let out' the engine at her full capacity downhill or a speed of fully 40 mph would have been realised".[6] War overtook *John Anthony* at Eaton Hall and the locomotive remained in store until 1916 when it was moved to Ravenglass.

The construction of the Class 60 marked the end of main stream production in the Large Scale Model Shop at Northampton, however, three other locomotives are worthy of brief mention. In 1909 Greenly had designed a tank engine version of *Little Giant* – driven by a petrol engine! *Blacolvesley*, an elegant 4–4–4T was

Plate 6.5
A contrast in scale and style. In this picture, taken at Ravenglass about 1921, the Heywood locomotive *Ella* (on the right) dwarfs the scale model Class 60 "Pacific", now named *Colossus*.
(*Ravenglass & Eskdale Railway*)

built for Mr Bartholomew of Blakesley Hall and survives to this day at Lightwater Valley near Ripon. In 1920 the first of six Atlantics designed by Greenly but built by Albert Barnes of Rhyl for the Miniature Railway appeared. These became the "Albion" class but they may have given a good indication as to what Class 40 might have looked like! *Sutton Belle* and *Sutton Flyer* of the Sutton Coldfield Miniature Railway were essentially completed from Class 30 Atlantic parts and drawings.

Narrow Gauge Railways Ltd was formed with the idea of operating larger 15 inch gauge lines. The developments at Fairbourne and Ravenglass were to some extent to realise this and although the years 1915–1925 saw the Ravenglass & Eskdale Railway as a glorious amalgam of 15 inch gauge practice somehow the dream never became reality. The scale model "Atlantics" and even the "Pacific" were not up to the rigours of a timetabled service over 7 miles of severe gradients and Greenly, in designing his massive 2–8–2 *River Esk* in 1923, went back to the over–scale principles advocated by Sir Arthur Heywood.

Plate 6.6
Class 30 "Atlantic" *Sanspareil* at the Eskdale terminus in 1916. This locomotive had previously run at the Oslo Exhibition of 1914.
(Ravenglass & Eskdale Railway)

By the early twenties Bassett–Lowke had abandoned the production of 15 inch gauge equipment and their place, for continental exhibitions at least was taken by German suppliers, Bassett–Lowke again concentrating on small scale models of the highest quality.

The story of the Bassett–Lowke 15 inch gauge locomotives is a fascinating one and new information is always coming to light. The challenge posed by researching the history of, perhaps, fifteen small locomotives is a daunting one but the immense pleasure given by these locomotives over the years cannot be doubted. It is interesting to note how the influence of Bassett–Lowke has lingered on, the two 15 inch gauge railways which formed the centrepieces of the Garden Festivals at Liverpool (1984) and Gateshead (1990) being worthy successors to the mantle of "Miniature Railways of Great Britain".

References

1. Sir Arthur Heywood *Minimum Gauge Railways* 3rd Edition 1898
2. Sir Arthur Heywood *Minimum Gauge Railways* 3rd Edition 1898
3. *Model Railways and Locomotives* ed. Henry Greenly and W J Bassett–Lowke, February 1909
4. *Models, Railways and Locomotives* ed. Henry Greenly and W J Bassett–Lowke, December 1912
5. *Models, Railways and Locomotives* ed. Henry Greenly and W J Bassett–Lowke, December 1912
6. *Models, Railways and Locomotives* ed. Henry Greenly and W.T. Bassett–Lowke, November 1914

Table 6.1

Dimensions of 15 inch gauge locomotives of Class 10, 20, 30 and 60

	Class 10 Little Giant 4-4-2	Class 20 Improved Little Giant 4-4-2	Class 30 Sanspareil 4-4-2	Class 60 Colossus 4-6-2	Heywood Standard 0-6-0T Ella[3]
Year of introduction	1905	1912	1912	1914	1881
Length of engine & tender	14ft 1 1/2ins	14ft 9ins	16ft 9ins	18ft 2ins	8ft 8ins
Weight of engine & tender	1ton 12cwt	1ton 15cwt	2tons 5cwt	3tons 0cwt	3tons 15cwt
Driving wheel diameter	18ins	18ins	20ins[2]	20ins	13 1/2 ins
Cylinders (2)	3 3/8 x 6ins	3 9/16 x 6ins	4 1/8 x 6 3/4 ins[2]	4 3/8 x 6 3/4ins	4 7/8 x 7ins
Boiler	1ft 3in wide 5ft 5in long 37 tubes	1ft 6in wide 5ft 5in long 37 tubes	1ft 7in wide 6ft 6in long 41 tubes	1ft 7in wide 8ft 0in long 41 tubes	2ft 1in wide 6ft 6in long 57 tubes
Working pressure (psi)	120[1]	125	130	150	160

Notes:
1. Initially 110 psi but subsequently raised
2. "Synolda" had 19 inch driving wheels and cylinders of 4 inch diameter
3. Included for comparison

Table 6.2

**Outline of the careers of the
Bassett–Lowke 15 inch gauge locomotives of Class 10, 20, 30 and 60**

(* denotes locomotive still in existence, Sept 1991)

CLASS 10

No 10 *Little Giant**	built 1905, to Blackpool. 1910 renumbered no. 14 and renamed *Little Elephant* for Halifax Zoo Railway. Stored by Bassett–Lowke 1914–1923, rebuilt with new boiler in 1923 and sent to Sunny Vale Railway, Halifax named *Baby Bunce*. Moved to the North–East in 1953, acquired from South Shields fairground in 1964 by Tom Tate. Renamed from *Robin Hood* to *Little Giant* in 1965. 1980 purchased by John Henderson and located at Lightwater Valley, Ripon. 1991 undergoing firebox repairs.
No 11 *Mighty Atom**	built 1908, to Sutton Coldfield. Jun–Nov 1909 to Nancy as No 13 *Ville de Nancy* then back to Sutton Coldfield for 1910 season. 1919 to Southport, overhauled and renamed *Prince of Wales*. To Yarmouth Miniature Rly 1929, returned to Sutton Coldfield 1938. Last steamed in 1953 and currently in store at Oldbury.
No 12 *Entente Cordiale*	built 1909, to Nancy. Probably to Brussels 1910 and then to other continental exhibitions. Final fate unsure, there are persistent rumours of the remains of a Class 10 being found behind German lines after World War I.
No 13 *Ville de Nancy*	See No 11
No 14 *Little Elephant*	See No 10
No 15 *Red Dragon**	built 1909, to White City Exhibition. 1911 to Rhyl renamed *Prince Edward of Wales*. 1920 to Dreamland Rly, Margate. 1968 private ownership and 1976 some parts used to rebuild No 18. 1983 rebuilding commenced based on original wheels, frames and cylinders, returned to steam at Southport 1991.
No 16 *Green Dragon*	built 1909 for White City Exhibition but not used. Probably used on continental lines 1909–11 but subsequent history not accurately known.
No 17 *King Leopold/King Albert/King Edward*	these were the names given to the locomotives provided for the 1910 Brussels Exhibition. One was new, the other two were likely to have been No 12 and No 16. Their subsequent histories are not known.

| No 18 *George the Fifth** | built 1911, to Southport. 1913 to Rhyl thence 1922 Skegness, 1932 Southend, 1938 Belle Vue, Manchester where lay derelict from mid–Fifties. Rebuilt and restored to working order 1976, now based at Carnforth. |
| No 19 *Hungaria** | built 1912, to Luna Park Railway, Geneva carrying the name *Bert–Wynne*. 1913 to Budapest where noted complete in 1991. |

CLASS 20

No 20 un–named	built 1912, to King Rama VI of Siam.
No 21 *Prince of Wales**	built 1912, to Southport 1913. Carried a variety of names after arrival of No 11 in 1919, occasionally different ones on either side of the locomotive! Damaged by fire, rebuilt and named *King George* 1938. Sold in 1971 to Whorlton Lido Rly, Barnard Castle and to Lightwater Valley 1989.
No 22 *Prince Edward of Wales**	built 1915, to Fairbourne 1916. 1923 to Southport. Damaged by fire, rebuilt and renamed *Princess Elizabeth* 1938. Sold 1969, part of the McAlpine collection and based at Carnforth.

CLASS 30

No 30 *Synolda**	built 1912, to Sand Hutton Rly. 1922 disposed of as line regauged and not positively identified again until 1932 at Southend. 1938 Dunns of Bishop Auckland, 1942 Belle Vue, Manchester, where in 1950s ran as *Prince Charles*. Dismantled locomotive given to Ravenglass and Eskdale Railway Museum in 1978 and restored to working order.
No 31 *Sanspareil*	built 1913, Oslo Exhibition 1914, Ravenglass & Eskdale Railway 1915, scrapped 1926.
No 32 *Count Louis**	built 1923 for count Louis Zborowski's Highams Rly near Canterbury. Fairbourne 1925–1985. Now static exhibit Birmingham Railway Museum.

CLASS 60

| No 60 *John Anthony* | built 1914, Staughton Manor Rly. Trials at Eaton Hall July 1914 then stored. 1916 to Ravenglass and Eskdale renamed *Colossus*. Dismantled 1927 and parts used in building first *River Mite*. |

7 A reviewer reviews: railway publishing today

Arthur Lowe

Railway literature and railway museums inhabit the same province. Both serve to deepen our understanding of railways and increase our enjoyment of our hobby. Those who visit railway museums with serious purpose, be they lay observers or professional railwaymen, come to learn, compare and interpret the artefacts on display; they constitute an informed market for books and magazines which the publishers aim to supply. We have no generic name for these "customers". To the French they are "Les Amis des Chemins de Fer" but we seem to be too reserved to indulge in such passion and make do with the clumsy appellation "railway enthusiast" (the late P Ransome–Wallis failed to find acceptance for his suggested "railwayist"[1]).

That there is interaction between the curatorial and the publishing function is obvious. Without the archival resources of the museum the authors of books or articles would be deprived of an important source of information and illustration, while in turn their published researches may add to the store of knowledge in the museum's library. It is fitting, therefore, in a volume to celebrate the first sixteen years of the National Railway Museum that space should be found for consideration of recent trends in railway publishing. Naturally the major portion of the book trade is subservient to commercial pressures whereas a National Museum, caring for our patrimony, is only subject to such pressures at arm's length. Even in the world of book publishing there are exceptions, as shown by the work of the Railway Correspondence & Travel Society whose exhaustive researches by teams of dedicated and now elderly volunteers have produced studies of the locomotives of the pre–grouping companies which surely approach the definitive. Work such as this, though not commercial in the strict sense, is understood to be profitable in the long term. The titles are held in stock for many years and those in demand are reprinted, with revisions.

If a railway enthusiast had been asked twenty–five years ago if he thought that the steady flow of railway publications would continue at its contemporary rate almost certainly the prediction would have been of a long, slow decline. True, many important initiatives had brightened and enlarged the post–war publishing scene. The "Regional History" series produced by David & Charles was an example. In this series, only recently completed, railway development in Great Britain was discussed by geographical area rather than by pre–grouping railway company. In a wider field the great Cecil J Allen (himself a successor to E L Ahrons and W J Scott) had been joined by his son, G Freeman Allen and by O S Nock.

Technical aspects of locomotive design, never previously discussed in such detail in enthusiast literature, were revealed in the works of H Holcroft and E S Cox. And, significantly, photographic albums appeared led by "the master" Eric Treacy in 1949.[2]

Nevertheless it might reasonably have been presumed that a plateau, if not a peak, had been reached, for, with the impending demise of steam traction and in the aftermath of "Beeching", the readership for railway literature would have declined as the size of the system diminished and as a variety of traffics disappeared. Above all it would be the last breath of steam which, after a suitable period of nostalgic mourning, would surely presage the end of the hobby.

> "The steam locomotive, most noble–seeming of all
> man's mechanical creations, enthrals us by its presence,
> its patent honesty, its reliability, its capacity for
> overwork and its response to the human touch"

(W A Tuplin, 1952)

In the event, gloomy predictions of decline and fall have proved to be completely wrong. Railway publishing has burgeoned: the number of books (some of them reprints) produced each year has steadily increased while new periodical magazines continue to emerge, each hopeful of securing a niche in the market place.

Let us now assess the recent history of railway publishing in greater detail.

Much of what follows originates from the author's involvement with the Newsletter of the Friends of the National Railway Museum. The Friends were established in 1977 as a Charitable Trust with the primary aim of assisting the Museum to acquire and renovate objects relevant to the development of rail transport. Other aims, which are forwarded by the publication of a quarterly Newsletter, are to keep members in touch with events in the Museum and to encourage the study of transport history. In November 1979 the Newsletter carried its first book review; since then nearly 500 have appeared in its pages – a fairly large sample of the books published over the last twelve years but not, it should be emphasized, a fair sample. Although the Friends receive a good proportion of the production of the major railway publishing houses, there are some who rarely send a review copy and then only because the author of the book, being a Friend, has requested it. Some, admittedly minor, publishers have never submitted a book for review. In contrast, from time to time, a review may appear of a book which a reviewer has bought on his own account and considers to be worthy of notice.

The growth of the review section of the Newsletter, to the extent that more than a dozen books are dissected for readers edification in each issue, has been achieved because the editors have been fortunate to find within the membership a number of well–informed and literate individuals to undertake the work. Some of the reviewers are authors in their own right. Books are allocated according to the known predilections of the reviewer, though sometimes a glance at the "acknowledgements" warns that the editor's first choice would be inappropriate! Gratifyingly, the impartiality and thoroughness of Newsletter reviews was acknowledged by Michael Harris, then Executive Director of Ian Allan Ltd, when he spoke on "Railway publishing" at a York evening meeting of the Friends in October 1988 (reported in the February 1989 Newsletter). In the following May there was a thoughtful article by Gordon Biddle on the same subject, which inspired in the August issue four letters to the editor, including a further contribution from Michael Harris. Whenever appropriate, points raised in the above discussion have been incorporated in this.

In considering the books reviewed over the past twelve years the most striking change has been the rise in the proportion of books in which illustration has taken a dominant position. Such books may be picture albums, pure and simple, or books, very often in a series, having a high pictorial content. Picture albums, as already noted, have been part of the post–war scene for many years; the uniform series published by Bradford Barton had achieved a century of titles by 1977. Since then other publishers, established and also newcomers, have exploited the genre. They have been encouraged by the collections of older photographs which have become available (often after the demise of the photographer) and by a host of newcomers producing work of the good technical quality which modern emulsions permit. This improvement is most marked in colour work which benefits also from the introduction of laser technology in the block–making process.

In books of the picture album sort the text is confined to the captions (perhaps after a short introductory chapter). At their worst the captions may tell us that the locomotive or train has been "caught by the camera" – a redundancy surely – or may indulge in the pathetic fallacy of "poses for the camera". Where extended captions are employed the standard is usually higher. Examples of informative captioning are to be seen in the volumes prepared posthumously from Eric Treacy's photographs by Whitehouse and Freeman Allen[3] and Jenkinson and Whitehouse,[4] notably in the latter instance, where the compilers have found details of the locomotive and coaching stock depicted, of which, one feels sure, the good bishop was blissfully oblivious! Another good series, this time captioned by the photographer himself, are the late Ivo Peter's volumes on the Somerset & Dorset in the fifties and sixties (recently reissued).

The production of picture books in a large format is particularly associated with the Oxford Publishing Company. In the earlier part of the period reviewed, they produced series of albums of locomotive photographs under the titles "The power of ......" and "Profile of ......". Some of these have been reprinted more recently "dot for dot", ie without updating the captioning. Other albums have presented the work of lesser known photographers. Though the pictures and captions have been of variable quality these seem to sell well and give enjoyment to many.

Mention has already been made of books "having a high pictorial content". It is the growth of this type which was the outstanding feature of the period. The publishing initiative of Ian Allan pioneered a blend of main text and fully captioned pictures exemplified by the late Brian Haresnape's series on the locomotives of prominent Chief Mechanical Engineers. First published c.1970, the series was added to, reprinted and revised throughout the eighties. When first issued they were described as "Pictorial Histories" but this apt description was dropped from later issues. Other examples of the format from this important publisher include the *BR Diary* set (3 volumes each covering a decade from 1948–77) and the *Rail Centres* series. This covers the country from Brighton to Edinburgh in, at the last count, sixteen books and each summarizes and comments upon the railway development and traffic of the designated "Centre".

Very successful, in commercial terms, has been a handsome succession of large format books from David & Charles; the first was *The Great Western Railway – 150 Glorious Years* followed by *The Great Days of the Country Railway*. Later members celebrated other sesquicentenaries. These books are team efforts. Their novelty lies in their design. A sequence of major and minor articles, distinguished by typeface as well as length, are interspersed with good photographs and drawings. Boxed "snippets" share the generous margins of the main articles with italicised captions to the illustrations. The relaxed layout is in tune with the nostalgic text and one is not surprised to note that they carry a fairly high cover price. Those who bought them when first published may, however, be dismayed to find them on offer, drastically reduced, as part of a Book Club package.

Ian Allan produced, in the early eighties and in a large format, the "..... At Work" books. In each of these, chapters on the engineering design of a class, or cognate classes, of locomotives were interspersed with sequences of photographs showing the locomotives in action (or at least in active service). Members of the curatorial staff at the National Railway Museum were responsible for two of the series.[5,6]

Other varieties of books relying heavily on illustration for their impact are the so–called encyclopaedias[7] and, of course, volumes on railway art, architecture, archaeology or artefacts which, by their nature, demand a pictorial approach. There have been several good examples in recent years.[8,9,10,11] Then there are the "coffee table" travel books with a strong railway theme such as Patrick and Maggy Whitehouse's *China by Rail* which must stand for several others, whereas *Great Railway Stations of Europe* was outstanding for its photography if not for all its factual detail.[12]

Before leaving the subject of illustrated books, it has to be recorded with sorrow that, in otherwise well–presented publications, it is possible to encounter examples of what – in a record photograph – is a heinous sin, namely the "cropping" of a chimney capuchon or a buffer. Infuriatingly, sometimes a feature pinpointed in a caption has been trimmed off the photograph before it appears on the printed page.

We must now turn our attention to the traditional or conventional railway books that have continued to appear in recent years. We define such traditional books as being those in which the written word is paramount and in which illustrations, if present, are used either to support the text or provide light relief from too solid a diet of words.

Despite constituting a lower proportion of the total, they have been quite numerous and present such variety of subject matter and style of approach as to defy simple classification. An enthusiast's bookshelf might display volumes ranging in subject from the biographies of the great and the good to the meticulous, anecdotal histories of obscure branches; from a critical assessment of accidents to a footplateman's reminiscences. Let us take these four genres as examples for the moment. Of the first there have been quite a few (and some of the auto–variety) but none to equal the style and thoroughness of those by L T C Rolt on the Stephensons and on Brunel except that on Daniel Gooch by Alan Platt.[13] Of the second, the David & Charles *Regional History* series has been completed and updated as have the companion *Railway Histories* as far as

Scottish Railways are concerned. Allen & Unwin produced slim three volume histories of three of the great railways in the relaxed style of their *Steam Past* series while Oakwood Press continued to publish new books on various minor railways and re–issue earlier ones. These last appeal to a serious, specialist market. Books from a recently retired professional investigator have enlivened the "accident" scene,[14,15] while, as was to be expected, the nostalgic memoirs of railwaymen (of all grades) have become quite numerous.

Books on train running over major routes have been cherished by railway enthusiasts for more than a century; the writings of Foxwell and Farrer and the great Ahrons are the "classics" of every good library. Their contemporary successors, notably Peter Semmens, until 1987 Assistant Keeper at the National Railway Museum, have continued the tradition, reporting and interpreting with scientific rigour on "practice and performance". The recent books on the developments on the East Coast Main Line by Semmens are especially worthy of mention.[16,17]

So much for "thematic" books; what of publications covering the field generally? To quite an extent these are now appearing as illustrated books and examples have already been noted, but for scholarship and style the best are still to be found under a "conventional" umbrella. They are not numerous. Three by the doyen of transport literature Jack Simmons, are outstanding,[18,19,20] well researched, indexed and with full bibliographies. A rare combination of practical engineering experience and familiarity with literary sources enlivens everything that Brian Hollingsworth writes, for example *Ffestiniog Adventure*[21] and that matchless bedside table book *The Pleasures of Railways.*[22]

Space does not permit us to discuss those books listing locomotive numbers and/or names, which have grown up from booklets to illustrated books; lists of preservation sites, railway maps (invaluable when accurate, infuriating otherwise), children's books and books of railway myth and legend, all of which have appeared and prospered during the period. And to be sure, apart from two passing references, we have focused on books about British railways, not only for considerations of space but also to be compatible with the main purview of the National Railway Museum. Travel on foreign railways has been the theme of several autobiographical odysseys, such as those by Paul Theroux and Colin Thubron but of these it may justly be said that they tell us more about their authors than railways. There does not seem to have been anything comparable from travellers on British (or indeed Western European) railways.

Lastly, there are the periodical magazines. Of these the commercial ones (as distinct from society journals) are all highly illustrated productions; indeed some have been launched on the basis of their pictorial content. They will be familiar to all railway enthusiasts and we shall refrain from invidious comparisons. Taking an overview, as the magazines fight out their battles on the bookstalls, one is impressed by the high quality of the articles which appear in many of them. This must reflect good editorial practice. What is surprising is that these standards do not invariably apply to the outpourings of the railway book trade. Of the 500 or so reviewed in the Friends' Newsletter over the years, several have been justly castigated, while two books were so bad that it was deemed unwise to print the reviewer's comments which were instead transmitted privately to the publisher. In a third, recent, instance the author of an unflattering review was protected by anonymity.

This sour note need not disturb our main conclusions, namely that railway publishing is flourishing and generally of good repute. We have seen that the growth area has been in illustrated books, especially where text and pictures are combined in an innovative way.

It is not easy to foresee what the future holds for railway publishing; the seductions of the video may make inroads in the popular market but for the discerning 'railwayist', books, supported by lively periodicals, will surely be indispensable for a long time to come.

References

1. P Ransome-Wallis, *On Railways,* Batchworth Press, 1951
2. E Treacy, *Steam Up,* Ian Allan, 1949
3. P B Whitehouse and G Freeman Allen, *Eric Treacy – Railway Photographer,* David & Charles, 1982
4. D Jenkinson and P B Whitehouse, *Eric Treacy's LMS,* Oxford Publishing Company, 1988
5. C P Atkins, *West Coast 4–6–0s at Work,* Ian Allan, 1981
6. M Rutherford, *Castles and Kings at Work,* Ian Allan, 1982
7. B Hollingsworth, *The Illustrated Encyclopaedia of the World's Steam Passenger Locomotives,* Salamander Books, 1982
8. B Cole and R Durack, *Happy as a Sand–Boy,* HMSO, 1990
9. G Biddle, *Great Railway Stations of Britain,* David & Charles, 1986
10. G Biddle, O S Nock, *The Railway Heritage of Britain,* Michael Joseph, 1983
11. P J G Ransom, *The Archaeology of Railways,* World's Work, 1981
12. M Binney and others, *Great Railway Stations of Europe,* Thames & Hudson, 1985
13. A Platt, *The Life and Times of Daniel Gooch,* Alan Sutton, 1987
14. S Hall, *Danger Signals,* Ian Allan, 1987
15. S Hall, *Danger on the Line,* Ian Allan, 1989
16. P Semmens, *Speed on the East Coast Main Line,* Patrick Stephens, 1990
17. P Semmens, *Electrifying the East Coast Route,* Patrick Stephens, 1991
18. J Simmons, *The Railway in England and Wales 1830–1914,* Leicester University Press, 1978
19. J Simmons, *The Railway in Town and Country 1830–1914,* David & Charles, 1986
20. J Simmons, *The Victorian Railway,* Thames & Hudson, 1991
21. B Hollingsworth, *Ffestiniog Adventure,* David & Charles, 1981
22. B Hollingsworth, *The Pleasures of Railways,* Allen Lane, 1983

8 Railway photography

Dick Riley

The early history of railway photography is well documented. Photography reached a state of greater availability in the mid 19th century although the equipment was generally heavy and cumbersome. Railway photographs taken in the late 1840s exist although not in the National Railway Museum collection. One depicts broad gauge locomotives outside the engine shed at Cheltenham. It is dated 1849 since the withdrawal of one of the engines in that year is well documented. Another famous photograph in the Victoria & Albert Museum Collection records the South Eastern Railway Crampton locomotive *Folkstone* on display at the Great Exhibition in 1851. The engine was built in that year although the town had been renamed Folkestone in 1844. Such photographs would have required bulky apparatus using glass plates, probably 15" x 12", needing to be sensitized on location, used while still wet and developed immediately in a portable darkroom.

Some early railway photographs show railway accidents. Railways were no longer news – railway accidents were. A photograph in the National Railway Museum Collection of the Great Western broad gauge engine *Lynx* derailed at Gatcombe near Lydney in 1852 is an example. The logistics of this exercise are worth a moment's thought. One assumes the photographer to have been a professional based in Lydney. First the news of the mishap would have to be conveyed to him by some means, then he would need to load his equipment on a horse–drawn conveyance. On arrival at the scene, having obtained the authority of a railway official, he would require assistance to lift his camera up the embankment, set it up on a tripod, sensitize, expose and develop the plate and then return to his studio. In later Victorian and Edwardian years photographers built up a steady trade in selling postcards of such events, which are now collectors' items. To put this in perspective it has to be remembered that national newspapers in this country had no photographic illustrations until early this century, the initiative belonging to the *Daily Mirror* in 1904.

The early camera could not record moving trains. Although most railways and locomotive builders began to employ official photographers, what passed for a moving train was often a stationary train posed at a suitably photogenic location. Pioneers in the field of works photographs were Messrs Beyer, Peacock of Manchester and fortunately their negatives are held in the local Museum of Science & Industry. The railway companies soon followed suit and many of their negatives – sadly by no means all – are held by the National Railway Museum. It was initially left to amateurs to record moving trains using a press camera equipped with a focal plane shutter permitting speeds of at least 1/500 second which had been available since the late 19th century. The limiting factor was the speed of the film used. The camera was still bulky and used on a tripod. Moreover the weight of the glass plates restricted the number that could be carried although by the latter part of the 19th century cameras were available to take quarter or half plate glass negatives, while sensitizing and developing on location was no longer necessary.

In general such cameras were used by comparatively wealthy enthusiasts usually having good connections with railway officers. Film speeds were low and often it was necessary to take a time exposure by the simple expedient of removing and replacing the lens cap. The right time was learned by experience – there were no such things as exposure meters.

There was a great advance in amateur photography at the turn of the century due largely to the availability of improved and more reliable glass plates with greater sensitivity to different colours, *ie* a bright red bufferbeam would be depicted in a different shade on a black and white print. Better quality lenses were also available and by this time more people were taking photographs, Eastman Kodak having introduced roll film so that it was no longer necessary to carry heavy photographic equipment.

Around the turn of the century and up to the Great War many railway companies produced their own postcards. These were not confined to railway views although many did depict railways. For some years railway company photographers had been recording scenes of places served by the railway, notably holiday resorts. Such scenes replaced advertisements in passenger compartments. Thus although advertising revenue was lost the railways benefited from increased tourism. Such pictures reproduced as postcards profited the railway companies from the publicity gained. Leader in the field was the London & North Western, which is said to have sold twelve million cards in about ten years at two old pence for six. The fact that postage on a postcard was half that of a letter and delivery just as quick ensured their success.

A further photographic development took place in 1925. At this time a British made Thornton Pickard reflex camera with f4.5 lens cost £12.0.0. In that year the first Leica 35mm cameras were imported from Germany at a cost of £22.0.0 including leather case. These cameras had very high resolution lenses, which if used with the fine grain film then available, could produce enlargements approaching the quality of those obtained from glass plates. Such is the subsequent amount of inflation it is now hard to believe that such cameras were only available to those of reasonable means, many photographers' early efforts being with a Box Brownie or Vest Pocket Kodak (VPK) folding camera. Better folding cameras such as those by Agfa, Voigtlander or Zeiss were imported from Germany before World War II. These used the once familiar and still available 120 size film providing eight 6cm x 9cm negatives. Also available were Hasselblad, Rolleicord or Voigtlander single lens reflex cameras using 120 size film. These cameras mostly had synchro compur shutters with speeds to 1/500 second. Railway photography to an acceptable standard was thus within the reach of many more people.

In order to improve the standard of railway photography the late Maurice Earley formed the Railway Photographic Society in 1922, initially consisting of a dozen members. The Society circulated portfolios with members' prints, and criticism sheets to enable fellow members to express their views. This achieved a great deal to raise the standards of those taking part and by the time the Society closed over fifty years later, following the end of scheduled steam on British Railways, membership had increased to fifty five. Fortunately Maurice Earley's negatives survive in the National Railway Museum Collection as do those of several other distinguished members.

The 1939–45 War brought an end to authorized railway photography. Film rapidly became scarce so this edict was easily observed. On one occasion when the writer failed to do so he went to a Scarborough processor to collect the prints only to be told that conforming with regulations the developed film and negatives had been sent to the local Police Station. There the Chief Inspector administered a severe caution for having photographed the Easingwold Railway, 2 miles in length with one engine and one coach! After the war film was initially in short supply but by the late 1940s railway photography had achieved a large following. This coincided with the nationalization of the railways so that the old company liveries disappeared, long accepted practices were changed, unremunerative branch lines were closed and the first main line diesel locomotives had entered traffic.

Colour photography first became available in the mid 1930s with the slow and grainy Dufaycolor film of 6cm x 9cm size. After the war Kodachrome film became available for 35mm camera users with Ektachrome for the users of 35mm and larger cameras. Later other films became available and in 1961 Kodachrome, hitherto rated at the slow speed of 8 ASA became available at 25 ASA. Higher speed films were available but usually lacking the flexibility of the 25 ASA Kodachrome and tending towards graininess in the photographs. Much research work by film manufacturing companies has been undertaken since then in order to reduce the grain in higher speed black and white and colour films, since this detracts from the fine definition of the picture.

In recent years the proliferation of railway magazines with a pictorial bias and notably with colour content has helped to improve the standard and variety of railway photography. The amateur tends to start with purely static record photographs and with improving confidence and equipment progresses to train photography. More important is the record of a train in its setting. The railway fabric no longer has the relative permanence it once enjoyed – for example there are few places where semaphore signals survive. There are many places in Britain other than the Settle & Carlisle line or the West Highland Line where scenic locations abound although many fine locations exist abroad. That is not to overlook home ground. Not everyone lives within easy reach of a preserved steam railway or British Rail lines on which steam specials run. Hence it is a case of recording the modern image of BR when it becomes even more important to choose locations with care and to record the train in its environment.

The railway photographer now has a wide choice of cameras, both new and secondhand. While single lens reflex cameras providing twelve 6cm x 6cm negatives or ten 6cm x 7cm negatives on 120 size film are still available, 35mm photography now predominates with cameras largely of Japanese origin although several Leica models are available. Essential requirements are that the lens, shutter and viewfinder should be of good quality. Having acquired confidence in his equipment the photographer should study the various magazines and if so desired attempt more adventurous photographs than the traditional 3/4 front view. So far as adventurous – or atmospheric – photographs are concerned, North American magazines were ahead of their European counterparts although some of these have now made up for lost ground.

The accompanying illustrations were chosen at random from the National Railway Museum Collection, a blend of traditional photographs either official or amateur. Selected to illustrate certain points, they are not intended to favour any one railway company nor can they attempt to show the diversity of the National Railway Museum Collection of 750,000 negatives, not all of which have been printed or are immediately available. Nevertheless, the prints in the Collection can be seen on weekdays preferably by prior appointment in the National Railway Museum reference library.

Plate 8.1
C Hamilton Ellis in his classic work *The Trains we loved* comments: "Many of the old companies used to decorate engines on special occasions and in the south of England particularly great heights of gaudy magnificence were attained with the royal train engines. The Brighton men were the masters of this pleasantly garish custom. Not only royalties were thus honoured, terrific effects were achieved in dressing engines for the annual staff outings". While the LBSCR may have had the edge this record of GNR 0–4–2 No. 70 adorned for the Hitchin Engineers Department outing in 1887 shows that the northern companies were not far behind. The engine is of interest in having been built as a 2–2–2 in 1850, rebuilt to this form in 1870 and surviving for another thirty years.

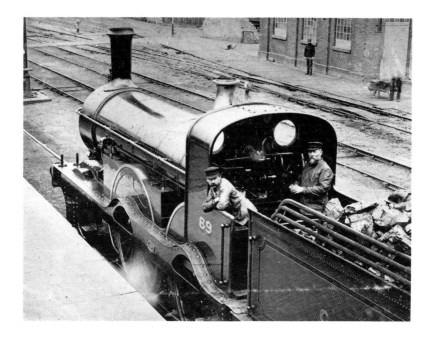

Plate 8.2
Among the early amateur photographers was P J Pilcher, whose negatives in the National Railway Museum Collection date back to 1882. He had clearly advised the footplatemen to keep still as the fact that this was a long exposure is shown by the drifting of steam and the 'ghosting' of the labourer with the wheelbarrow at right. The engine is GNR Stirling 2–4–0 No. 89 built in 1874 and recorded at Boston in 1889. Following rebuilding in 1898 it survived until 1913.

Plate 8.3
Official works photographs often tended to emphasize the locomotive to the exclusion of its surroundings. Often this was done by meticulous retouching of the large glass plate negative. In this case on a 15" x 12" glass plate the effect has been achieved by photographing the engine against a large sheet of calico draped from a building at Crewe Works. The engine is an 0–6–2T with 5'0" driving wheels for passenger work, LNWR No. 1597 built in 1898 which survived until 1947 as LMSR No. 6870.

Plate 8.4
This picture is a comparison showing different ideas being a later Crewe Works picture taken in more picturesque surroundings on the Chester line. It is a picture tinged with regret as it depicts the last surviving LNWR express passenger locomotives after withdrawal in 1949, none being preserved. This resulted in the 1891 2–4–0 *Hardwicke* being the most modern LNWR passenger engine in the National Railway Museum, its claim to fame resulting from the rivalry between East and West Coast routes and the 1895 high speed runs to the north in which *Hardwicke* made outstanding runs between Crewe and Carlisle. Those illustrated are 'Precursor' 4–4–0 No. 25297 *Sirocco* (1904), rebuilt 'Claughton' 4–6–0 No. 6004 (1920/rebuilt 1928) and 'Prince of Wales' 4–6–0 No. 25752 (1919). Before going for scrap they were shunted into this position by a Stanier Class 8F 2–8–0 to be recorded by the works photographer.

Plate 8.5
There are some photographs depicting locomotives preserved in the National Railway Museum Collection of which this is an example. It shows the elegant Wainwright Class D 4–4–0 No. 737 passing Charing on the Maidstone–Ashford line conveying the Shah of Persia to Dover Harbour after a 1902 state visit. Note the whitewashed coal, a feature of such events at the time. Charing station is little changed apart from the loss of its goods yard, a 1964 victim of Dr Beeching's cuts.

Plate 8.6
A group photograph of station staff at the SER station at Canterbury, now the West station, towards the end of the 19th century. One assumes that all shifts were present but even so it seems a generous provision compared to today's standards. It features long forgotten occupations such as wheeltappers and the inevitable enamel advertisements. The almost concealed engine was Stirling F Class 4–4–0 No. 20 built in 1888. No doubt this scene was recorded by a local professional photographer, probably using a whole plate glass negative. This print has been copied onto a film negative.

Plate 8.7

A remarkably well–defined photograph of Brighton engine shed on a Sunday afternoon. The photographer, G F Burtt, appears to have warned the staff by the water tank since they are waiting expectantly. The Stroudley 'Terrier' 0–6–0T No. 671 *Wapping* was sold to the Kent & East Sussex Railway in 1905, while the Billinton Class E5 0–6–2T No. 572 *Farncombe* was not built until 1903 thus effectively establishing the date. Again the action of the steam on some of the locomotives indicates a small camera aperture combined with a slower shutter speed. G F Burtt worked in Brighton Works as a premium apprentice; he used a half plate camera.

Plate 8.8

The Lancashire & Yorkshire fire train gives a demonstration of its powers at Horwich Works in December 1915. The low lighting of winter sunshine brings out all the detail. L&YR 2–4–2T No. 733 in charge eventually became LMS No. 10820. Remarkably there is a 1949 picture of the fire train in charge of BR No. 50646, an older member of the same class. The water tank wagon was still in use but the pump by then was housed in a former LNWR bogie luggage van.

Plate 8.9

This is an example of an official photograph of a Midland Railway train which would leave you to believe that it was moving, whereas in fact it is standing still as the slight drift of smoke from the chimney indicates. The engine is No. 451 built in 1894 as reboilered in 1906. Since it was never superheated it was withdrawn twenty years later. The station building was one of Francis Thompson's best designs for the 1840 North Midland Railway at Ambergate. It was replaced by a new station in 1863 on a different site. A listed building, it survived into early BR days but regrettably was demolished.

Plate 8.10

The Midland Railway had expansionist ideas and turned up in the most unlikely places. Class 3F 0–6–0 No. 43277 was working a Hereford–Brecon train near Three Cocks Junction in May 1952. By this time the line came under Western Region control hence the use of GWR carriages. This photographer, J H Russell Smith, found the most scenic locations and this is no exception. The train is probably the 12.42pm as the high sun in a cloudless sky inevitably loses any detail below the frames. A few white fleecy clouds can help diffuse the light in such a situation but with the disadvantage that one may obscure the sun at the crucial moment that the train is passing. On a line with so sparse a timetable there was no second chance.

Plate 8.11

With the impending demolition of Euston station the railway's official photographer recorded the scene at the arrival and suburban departure side as it was in 1960. The resulting picture with its sweeping curve makes some impact. Although this scene does not survive there are many BR stations worthy of being recorded photographically, a large number of them being Listed Buildings.

Plate 8.12
A 'Metro' 2–4–0T No. 628 heads a Cheltenham–Kingham train near Charlton Kings in 1924. These engines were so–called because of their association with Metropolitan Railway lines for which purpose those so employed were fitted with condensing apparatus. No. 628 was never so equipped. Built in 1871 it survived until 1930 and Humphrey Household recorded it on a plate glass negative.

Plate 8.13
Apart from his photograph work while at Cambridge University and some excellent Canadian shots the majority of G H Soole's photographs – all on glass plates – were taken near his Bristol home. Whilst he mostly recorded passenger trains he did not neglect the all important freight. This photograph shows GWR 2–8–0 No. 2819 heading a down mixed freight and empty van train at Brent Knoll, near Weston super Mare, in the late 1930s. Points to note are the lack of foliage on the trees indicating a low sun giving excellent side lighting, the wind is blowing the steam in the right direction and the coupling rods are down. This latter point was easier to achieve on a slow freight train than on an express. Nevertheless these heavy goods engines with their 4' 7½" driving wheels could achieve a fair turn of speed.

Plate 8.14
The majority of Maurice Earley's photographs were taken within easy reach of his Reading home, notably between Twyford and Tilehurst, with Sonning Cutting, now densely overgrown, his favourite location because it provided a natural windshield so avoiding the problem of steam drifting down. His negative register was a model of its kind quoting not only the locomotive number, identity of train, place, date and time but also the weather conditions and details of development of the plate. This photograph depicts GWR 'Star' Class 4–6–0 No. 4023 *Danish Monarch* heading an up Fishguard boat express at Twyford, August 1933. Many railway photographers remember Maurice with gratitude for his inspiration in introducing the photographic portfolios.

Plate 8.15

A consistently good amateur photographer was A L P Reavil; his SR and GWR negatives are in the National Railway Museum Collection, those of the LMS and LNER in private hands. He frequently contributed to the staff magazines of the period which may indicate how he came to be in possession of a lineside track pass. A look-out man frequently appears in his photographs as in this example. Built twelve years before No. 737, Stirling 4–4–0 SR No. A 194 was among the last survivors of the unreboilered F Class and was withdrawn from Ramsgate shed in 1926. It is seen leaving Folkestone Junction on an Ashford–Ramsgate train. The station was renamed Folkestone East in 1962 but closed three years later. Largely demolished it still sees occasional use as a staff halt.

Plate 8.16

When the negative collection of A Halls was advertised Maurice Earley bought fifty and Roger Sellick a similar number and these are in the National Railway Museum Collection. It would be interesting to know if several hundred others survive, although this is doubtful. This is a truly post grouping Southern Railway picture by A Halls. It depicts ex LBSCR Class E1/R 0–6–2T No. B94, built as an 0–6–0T in 1883 and rebuilt by the SR in 1927 with a trailing pony truck, enlarged cab and increased coal bunker capacity, one of ten so converted for use on West Country branches. It is standing at Instow on a Torrington–Barnstaple train consisting of a guard's van of LCDR origin and two LSWR carriages.

Plate 8.17

Frank Box was a Guildford bank manager who submitted many prints and articles to the *Southern Railway Magazine* as a result of which he probably had prior advice of any unusual workings. Hence he was at Waterloo on 13 June 1939 to record 'Lord Nelson' Class 4–6–0 No. 851 *Sir Francis Drake* leaving on the 2.54pm semi fast train to Basingstoke, at that time more likely to have been hauled by a 4–4–0. In fact the engine had been overhauled and repainted in readiness to work the Royal Train conveying Their Majesties King George VI and Queen Elizabeth from Southampton to Waterloo following their visit to Canada, this taking place on 22 June. Hence the working of the Basingstoke train was a gentle running in turn. Frank Box used a simple folding camera using 6cm x 9cm negatives.

Plate 8.18
The 'West Riding Limited' was the third streamlined train put into service by the LNER between 1935 and 1937. Thirty five of the famous Gresley Class A4 4–6–2s were introduced to work these and other top link express trains on the East Coast route. Here Cyril Herbert, never without his 35mm Leica camera while carrying out his duties as a Civil Engineer, recorded the up train south of Stevenage in charge of No. 4496 *Golden Shuttle*. This engine was renamed *Dwight D Eisenhower* in 1945 and is one of six of the class to survive in preservation, being housed at the National Railroad Museum of Green Bay, Wisconsin, USA.

Plate 8.19
Death of an A4. Built in March 1938 No. 4469 *Sir Ralph Wedgwood* was destroyed when York engine shed was bombed on 29 April 1942, no easy task for the official photographer to record. This is of significance in that the National Railway Museum is now housed on this site and is host to No. 4468 *Mallard*, also built in March 1938, which attained the world speed record for a steam engine of 126mph in July 1938. The tender of No. 4469 survived although it must have been substantially rebuilt. The location of 4469 at the time of the bombing is now marked by a plaque on the floor of the Great Hall of the Museum.

Plate 8.20
An almost forgotten scene recorded by R D Stephen as a typical Scottish 'Pug Tank', LNER No. 10101, the first of a class of 35 engines built for the NBR between 1882 and 1899, works a transfer trip between Portobello and Lochend freight yards near Craigentinny in 1926. All but two of these powerful little engines survived into BR ownership, the last being withdrawn in 1962. The coal bunker capacity was so small that these engines were permanently coupled to primitive wooden 'tenders' to augment the coal supply.

Plate 8.21
A record shot of an express train scheduled to be hauled by a veteran tank engine but nevertheless a nicely lit picture with some impact. Recorded by a local press photographer, H L Overend, it depicts ex GNR Class N1 0–6–2T No. 69471 hauling the Bradford portion of the up 'Queen of Scots' Pullman train at Laisterdyke in the early 1950s. The 'Queen of Scots' in post war years was a ten coach train between London and Leeds, eight coaches forming the Edinburgh portion and two coaches thence to Bradford. The Gresley brake coach was presumably added to make up for the lack of guard's accommodation in the Pullman cars. This engine had also had some association with Metropolitan Railway lines since the condensing pipes indicate that it had once worked in the London surburban area.

Plate 8.22
To bring this collection up to date, the final
plate commemorates the formal opening of
the enlarged National Railway Museum on
16 April 1992, by HRH The Duke of Kent.
The Duke is seen on that occasion on the
footplate of the Museum's prime working
exhibit, *Duchess of Hamilton*.

9 Railway preservation in the 1920s and 1930s

Dieter W Hopkin

The number of important relics preserved by British railway companies prior to the grouping of 1923 cannot be considered a balanced or systematic collection representing the development of railway transport. Even in terms of locomotives, early examples had been lost to the scrap yards. One author has referred to an "... indifference to the fate of historic engines ... typical of most railways in the pre–grouping era".[1] There were fundamental problems for any organized preservation due to the structure of the railway industry. The great number of operating companies made any attempt at comprehensive collection extremely difficult. Co–operation to preserve examples of defunct machinery was unlikely in a commercial atmosphere in which companies were often bitter rivals. There was no central agency to act as a focus to co–ordinate the piecemeal efforts made in local areas. This contrasts sharply with the development of railway museums in Europe which were facilitated by the central direction provided by state–owned railways. Furthermore, there appears to have been a paucity of public or professional interest in the preservation of railway material. As W O Skeat points out: "In general, you will find very little in the way of published appeals for locomotive preservation until the first decade of the 20th century and indeed it was not until the 1920s that a significant amount of attention was given to the subject".[2]

Two major factors influenced a change in attitude during the 1920s and 1930s; the formation of the Big Four railway companies and the rash of railway centenaries celebrated during this period. The amalgamation of the plethora of railway companies to create the Big Four grouping [Great Western Railway (GWR), London, Midland & Scottish Railway (LMS), London & North Eastern Railway (LNER) and the Southern Railway (SR)] under the 1921 Railways Act brought about a great rationalization of the organization of Britain's railway transport. Created in 1923, the new companies sought to forge their new identities and an appreciation of railway history was seen as a useful aid in achieving this. An historical perspective was much easier to achieve after 1923 as railway history could then be simply divided into the sum of events and achievements which led to the formation of each of the four new companies. Greater centralization also provided an opportunity for a preservation policy to be developed and material drawn together from throughout a large operating region. The celebration of railway centenaries which began in 1925 with that of the opening of the Stockton & Darlington Railway provided a convenient platform to review railway development. The 1925 celebrations awakened public awareness of Britain's railway past and "turned the spotlight of nationwide publicity on the railway past ... and many relics of the pioneering days were displayed to the public for the first time".[3]

The most popular part of the celebrations of July 1925 was an exhibition of more than 100 locomotives and other rolling stock at Faverdale Wagon Works,

Darlington and a procession on part of the Stockton & Darlington line. A cavalcade of locomotives and rolling stock spanning the century was gathered together by the LNER. It featured locomotives preserved by railway companies some of which, like the Hetton Colliery locomotive of 1822 and the S&DR 0–6–0 *Derwent* of 1845, were restored to working condition. S&DR *Locomotion No. 1* was not considered suitable for steaming but took its part in the procession powered by a concealed internal combustion engine.[4] Lacking any locomotive to represent its early engineering practice the Great Western Railway exhibited a replica of the 2–2–2 locomotive *North Star* which incorporated parts of the original 1837 locomotive, scrapped in 1906, retrieved by souvenir hunters at Swindon. The construction of this replica has been regarded by some as partial expiation for the destruction of the original locomotive in 1906 but what appears more likely is that the management of the GWR realized the publicity value of an "old timer" in developing its corporate image.

Plate 9.1
Line-up of historic locomotives at the Stockton & Darlington Railway Centenary Celebrations at Darlington, July 1925. At the front is the Hetton Colliery 0-4-0 locomotive (1822), followed by Stockton & Darlington Railway 0-6-0 *Derwent* (1845), then North British Railway 0-6-0 No. 38 (1867) and Stockton & Darlington Railway 0-6-0 No. 1275 (1874) *(NRM)*

The assembled exhibits at Darlington formed the largest collection of historic rolling stock ever seen. The exhibition and cavalcade focused on historic items but also included some of the finest examples of contemporary practice. Exhibits were mostly gathered from the LNER with motive power ranging from Sentinel–Cammell steam railcars to Gresley's 2–8–8–2 Garratt. The other Big Four companies were also represented as were pioneers of the Belgian State Railways and the Netherlands. Goods and passenger rolling stock was also displayed as well as a substantial collection of small relics and documents.[5]

The authorities which gathered together this large collection of exhibits attest a clear sense of historical perspective and understanding of contemporary railway practice. The selection was heavily biased towards locomotives, as had all railway preservation in Britain been to date. However, significant examples of other material were included. The European exhibits also demonstrate an appreciation of the impact of the locomotive overseas.

A modern preservationist may look back on lists of exhibits assembled with regret that a collection of such wealth could not have been kept together for permanent preservation. Some were to be preserved in the LNER's proposed York railway museum, other examples have been set aside in more recent times, but notable types have been totally lost leaving significant historic and technological gaps in the collection which represents Britain's railway history.

A rival to the North Eastern celebrations were those commemorating the opening of the Liverpool & Manchester Railway in 1830. Though not on such a grand scale (with only 34 vehicles) the festivities at Liverpool in September 1930 show clear parallels with those five years earlier. There were again two main elements, an exhibition of historical material relating to the evolution of railways assembled in St George's Hall, Liverpool and the "Great Railway Fair" at Wavertree Playground. The latter was an exhibition of rolling stock which included a replica of Stephenson's *Rocket*, the two LNWR veteran 2–2–2s *Columbine* and *Cornwall*, examples of other LMS pre–grouping locomotives and a representative modern express passenger locomotive from each of the Big Four companies. There were also four examples of British railway export engineering with two locomotives each from the Leeds firm of Hunslet and Bagnall of Stafford. A selection of contemporary rolling stock was also shown.

Plate 9.2
London & North Western Railway 2-2-2 *Cornwall* and Midland Railway 4-2-2 No. 118 at the Liverpool & Manchester Railway Centenary Exhibition at Wavertree Park, Liverpool, September 1930. *(NRM)*

The centrepiece of the "Railway Fair" was undoubtedly the restored Liverpool & Manchester Railway (L&MR) 0–4–2 locomotive *Lion* (1838) which, hauling a rake of replica L&MR coaches, afforded to visitors "the unique educational experience of travelling ... under precisely the same conditions as the first railway passengers experienced".[6]

Plate 9.3
Liverpool & Manchester Railway 0-4-2 *Lion* and a train of replica coaches giving "...the same conditions as the first railway passengers experienced". Wavertree Park, Liverpool, September 1930. *(NRM, Nevitt Collection)*

The preservation of *Lion*, a locomotive which had spent most of its working life as a stationary boiler in the service of the Mersey Docks & Harbour Board, was a remarkable achievement as is outlined by Jarvis and Morris.[7] Perhaps the most significant features are the involvement of a public pressure group which actively campaigned for the preservation of this historic locomotive and its restoration to working order by the LMS. "Late in 1927, a number of members of the Liverpool Engineering Society, conscious of the recent centenary of the Stockton & Darlington Railway and anxious that the celebration of the centenary of the Liverpool & Manchester Railway should reflect the greater importance of the latter enterprise, began to look towards seeking *Lion's* restoration".[8] They formed the Old Locomotive Committee which eventually acquired the locomotive and made arrangements for refurbishing it at the LMS workshops at Crewe. This is a notable example of the successful use of external public pressure on one of the major railway operating companies to not only save but permanently preserve a locomotive. The restored *Lion* also proved useful to the LMS publicity department as its retirement to a plinth on Liverpool Lime Street Station was interrupted to take part in promotional events such as the London & Birmingham Railway centenary celebrations at Euston in 1938.[9]

The first example of private locomotive preservation was the Stephenson Locomotive Society's (SLS) acquisition of the London Brighton & South Coast Railway (LB&SCR) 0–4–2 *Gladstone*. This landmark in railway preservation was achieved under the influence of J N Maskelyne, president of the SLS. The proposal to preserve *Gladstone*, then recently withdrawn from service, was put to Society members early in 1927 on the basis that the locomotive represented "the unique achievement of a unique locomotive engineer whose influence upon locomotive engineering generally can still be noted at the present time". A successful appeal raised funds to purchase the locomotive and restore it to its LB&SCR livery.

From the beginning of this venture it had been intended that the locomotive should be housed in a museum. The Society hoped that it could be accommodated in the Science Museum, South Kensington, but as space was not available it was placed, with the approval of the LNER, in their museum at York.[10] This pioneering effort by the SLS marked the beginning of the Society's considerable involvement in railway preservation which became very significant in the 1950s.

The railway companies were not totally indifferent to the fate of veteran items of rolling stock. The two examples above indicate that they responded to public lobbying. Within the companies there were those who sought to save relics of a changing industry. Derby locomotive works, the former Midland Railway's nerve centre, began under the LMS an enlightened preservation programme in 1926 when one of Kirtley's double–framed 0–6–0s of 1856 was laid aside. It was repainted in Midland Railway (MR) livery and given its old number, 421. By 1930, 421 had been joined by four other locomotives: ex MR 4–2–2 No. 118, ex North London Railway 4–4–0T No. 6445, ex MR Kirtley double–framed 2–4–0 No. 156A and Johnson's first 0–4–4T No. 6. All underwent at least cosmetic restoration and in January 1931 they were moved into the works paint shop, which was designated as the unofficial museum.[11] There they might have expected a fairly untroubled future, being pulled out for various publicity or filming events, had not the new Chief Mechanical Engineer, W A Stanier, considered them a luxury which could not be afforded and directed that all be cut up and scrapped with the sole exception of No. 118. Only one example of the historic types destroyed in 1932 has since been preserved; ex MR Kirtley double–framed 2–4–0 No. 158A which was laid aside in Derby works in 1947.[12]

Plate 9.4
Midland Railway 0-4-4T No. 6 as restored in the Derby works paint-shop circa 1930. Also stored at Derby (behind No. 6) at that time was the *Rocket* replica used by the London, Midland & Scottish Railway at publicity events. *(Courtesy R.J. Essery)*

Plate 9.5
London & North Western Railway 18" gauge 0-4-0ST *Pet* laid aside for preservation in Crewe works paint-shop, 18 August 1935. *Cornwall* can also be seen in the background. *(NRM, Mullett Collection)*

Stanier's reason for purging the Derby paintshop appears similar to that of Churchward at Swindon a quarter of a century earlier; that the locomotives were taking up valuable workshop space. This need for thrift and careful management of resources must have been emphasized in the difficult financial atmosphere of the 1930s and paintshop "museums" made no direct economic contribution to running a railway. Although these were the harsh economic facts the paintshop at Derby works cannot have been of paramount operational importance as changes in workshop and maintenance practices meant that by the 1930s locomotives were no longer closeted for a week or more while elaborate liveries were applied. To a large extent paintshops became redundant. The works paintshop was therefore frequently the place for large relics to be laid aside not only at Derby but also at Crewe, which at this date housed a collection of London & North Western Railway locomotives including the 2–2–2s *Columbine* and *Cornwall*, the 2–4–0 *Hardwicke* and the narrow gauge 0–4–0ST *Pet*. The Crewe collection was threatened with the same fate as that at Derby but intense worker reaction caused a change of heart.[13] At Eastleigh on the Southern Railway an extensive collection of small relics and machinery was assembled by the Works Process Engineer.[14] What may have been more influential in Stanier's thoughts was that the collection at Derby was apparently the product of a purely local initiative involving mainly locomotives from the Midland Railway. It therefore represented a clinging to a pre–grouping company which was incompatible with the modern corporate image of the LMS in the 1930s. This does not, however, explain why the Crewe collection was allowed to survive.

A further example from the LMS serves to illustrate that although companies would lay important items aside for preservation there was little support for projects which involved financial outlay.

The LMS was lobbied by interested parties during the 1930s for the preservation of pre–grouping locomotive types due for withdrawal. Two particular candidates were the ex–L&NWR 2–4–0 *Hardwicke* and ex–Caledonian Railway 4–2–2 No. 123 which were officially preserved by the LMS in 1932 after pleas in the railway press and by interested individuals. One of these, Rev R B Fellows, enquired about the official policy of the LMS on the preservation of historic material. He received a reply from Sir Harold Hartley, Vice–President of the LMS, which stated: "..... that the policy of his own company is to preserve anything that may be of interest, in the hope that in more prosperous days it might be possible to assemble the exhibits in some central museum; the great thing was to save them from destruction". Sir Harold added that the LMS would be glad to co–operate when funds were available, but it was a bad time to get money for any such scheme as this.[15] It is unfortunate that Sir Harold Hartley failed to inform William Stanier of his company's policy!

Rev Fellows put forward ideas for a co–ordinated scheme for preservation by the railway companies and established museums to the newly created Standing Committee on Museums and Galleries. While he appears to have briefly considered the possibility of a central museum of railways, this was dismissed as impractical due to the scattering of preserved locomotives and other artefacts at many diverse locations. What he suggested as an alternative was: "the completion of a list showing what railway exhibits actually exist and where they are to be seen".[16] The Standing Committee referred this suggestion to Sir Henry Lyons, Director of the Science Museum, who in turn passed it on to the principal railway companies who expressed a willingness to co–operate with such a project so far as their own holdings were concerned. Unfortunately this potentially valuable scheme proceeded no further due to the unwillingness of anybody to fund it. Had it gone forward it might have recorded the official but private collections such as that of the GWR at Paddington Station, that of the LMS at Euston and the unofficial collections stored in paintshops and other backwaters which were later dispersed or destroyed.[17]

Although there was no clear support for a national railway museum, or even a catalogue of potential exhibits, in the 1930s Britain's first major railway museum was established at York. It had its origins in the North Eastern Railway, which was to lose its identity under the Railways Act (1921) becoming part of the larger LNER. As a response to this "some of the officers of the old company, at York felt an understandable anxiety that precious relics and traditions of the railway might be lost in the process".[18] J B Harper, Assistant Superintendent at York, began a collection of railway relics at York which was granted formal recognition when he was invited to chair a committee: "for cataloguing and bringing together where practicable, books, plans and objects of historical interest concerned with the North Eastern Railway".[19]

Formal collecting revealed a significant amount of material within the company's network which related to the early years of the NER and even of the Stockton & Darlington Railway. After the grouping, collecting widened to cover the whole of the LNER network. Small items were entrusted to the care of E M Bywell who placed them in a basement room at the railway offices at York "fitted out for their safe storage".[20] Some of these items were exhibited at the Stockton & Darlington Railway celebrations of 1925. In preparation for the cavalcade a number of locomotives were laid aside and restored "to something like their original condition".[21] With large and small relics assembled and national public interest stimulated the atmosphere was fertile for the establishment of a museum by the LNER in the North East. After some debate as to the respective merits of Darlington and York the latter location was selected for Britain's first railway museum. After the celebrations of 1925 and with the proposed railway museum in mind the restored locomotives were housed in the former machine shops of the York & North Midland Railway locomotive works. Here the North Eastern specimens were joined in 1927 by the Stephenson Locomotive Society's *Gladstone* and the former Great Northern Railway (GNR) 4–2–2 No. 1. The preservation of GNR No. 1 and other locomotives from that company owed much to the efforts of H N Gresley, Chief Mechanical Engineer of the LNER, who had an enthusiasm for old locomotives which was unique amongst his contemporaries.[22] The railway museum at York had, therefore, support at the highest levels within the company. The locomotives formed the core of the large exhibits section while the two–dimensional and small objects were housed separately in the former First Class Refreshment Room at the Old Station.

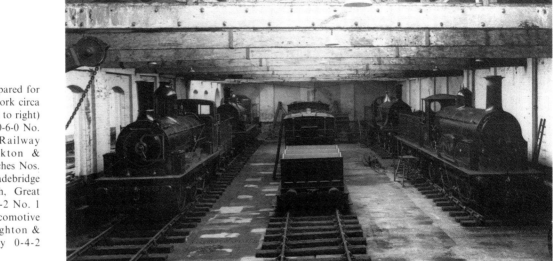

Plate 9.6
Large exhibits being prepared for the LNER museum at York circa 1927. They are (from left to right) North Eastern Railway 0-6-0 No. 1275, North Eastern Railway 2-4-0 No. 910, Stockton & Darlington Railway coaches Nos. 31 and 59, Bodmin & Wadebridge Railway third class coach, Great Northern Railway 4-2-2 No. 1 and the Stephenson Locomotive Society's London, Brighton & South Coast Railway 0-4-2 Gladstone. *(NRM)*

The date on which the museum at York was opened to the public is unclear, either 1927 or 1928, with a period of limited opening on application to the Curator prior to this. E M Bywell gathered together an increasing number of exhibits which he displayed in subject groups including trackwork, signalling and other topics as well as rolling stock. Although maintained and operated by the LNER, as the only major railway museum in Britain, items from the other major railway companies gravitated towards it. During the 1930s the large exhibits section expanded with major additions such as the GWR 4-4-0 *City of Truro* (1931), SR Bodmin & Wadebridge Railway coach (1932) and L&NWR 2-2-2 *Columbine* (1934). The Science Museum placed *Agenoria*, the Shutt End colliery locomotive, on loan in 1937. Further LNER locomotives were also added during the 1930s, including the NER Worsdell–Von–Borries compound *Aerolite* and GNR 4-4-2 *Henry Oakley*. The growth of the locomotive collection was paralleled by that of the small relics as items were drawn in from the LNER, other companies, and by the acquisition of a number of major private collections.

By the mid 1930s the York Railway Museum could be acclaimed as "probably the finest collection of historic engines in the world", and it is remarkable what had been achieved in the short period from 1922 with limited resources.[23] It is significant in that the NER and its successor the LNER showed what could be achieved if there was an official desire by a railway operating company to preserve its historic relics. The interest of Gresley and other senior officials in the company also led to preserved locomotives coming out from the museum to be put back into steam for publicity events such as the steaming of GNR 4–2–2 No. 1 which ran with a rake of restored six–wheeled coaches in 1938, to coincide with improvements in East Coast express running.[24] The LNER's York Museum, in the absence of any other, became *the* railway museum in Britain for the next 30 years.

In proposing his scheme for a railway relics catalogue, Rev Fellows listed three major public collections of railway material: "the Science Museum at South Kensington; the Railway Museum at York (and), the Transport Collection in the Hull Municipal Museum".[25] This last collection represents an interesting and unique concern for railway preservation shown by a local authority museum. This active interest by Hull Corporation museums was a product of the work of a remarkable man, Thomas Sheppard, their curator from 1900. In his curatorial work Sheppard was said to combine "..... the qualities of the dove, the serpent, the antiquarian and the buccaneer" and during his period as curator, and later director, he built up a network of museums in Hull which covered the whole spectrum of museum disciplines.[26] Sheppard was a former employee of the NER in Hull, so it is not surprising that he began collecting railway material and was assisted by his former colleagues in the local railway management.

Sheppard's railway collection was first placed on public display at the Museum of Commerce and Transport in the Old Corn Exchange opened in 1924.[27] The rapid growth of the collection meant that new accommodation had to be sought and following an agreement with the LNER space was provided in Hull Paragon Station. The new museum, the first "Railway Museum in a Railway Station", opened in 1938 and boasted over 2000 specimens. Most of the exhibits fell into the small relics category with the catalogue listing a large number of prints, watercolours, drawings and ephemera, a collection of models, railway pottery, stamps and a fine collection of railway heraldry. There were few large–scale exhibits with the exception of examples of permanent–way. Despite the local character of the Hull railway collection and the proximity of the LNER museum at York, Sheppard received donations from the major railway companies.[28] Perhaps the most remarkable acquisition was a Kitson tram locomotive from the LMS–owned Northern Counties Committee system in Ireland, which was donated to Hull after negotiation with the parent company.[29]

Sheppard was an avid collector and stands out as one of the remarkable museum characters of the inter–war period. The creation of the railway museum was a direct result of his work and finds no parallels in other local authority museums. Although the museum did not include any major items of rolling stock, it serves as an example of what could be achieved on a local basis even during a period of economic decline in the 1930s. Regrettably it is no longer possible to study his remarkable work as the museum and its collection was destroyed by a World War II bombing raid. Only a small fragment of the collection survives in the present Transport Collection of Kingston–upon–Hull museums.[30]

It is fortunate that amongst preserved railway material, direct victims of the hostilities of the Second World War are few. The Railway Museum at York was closed and the locomotive collection evacuated to various railway installations in the North East. Other exhibits were removed from their plinths: the former S&DR locomotives *Locomotion* and *Derwent* moved from Darlington to Stanhope in Weardale and *Lion* from Liverpool Lime Street to Crewe.[31,32] Bombing raids on the armaments factories at Barrow–in–Furness caused extensive damage to the station and blew the glass out of preserved Furness Railway 0–4–0 No 3's display case. The locomotive itself received only minor damage and was soon removed for safekeeping to Horwich locomotive works.[33] The City & South London Railway electric locomotive No. 36, which had been displayed on a plinth at Moorgate Station since 1938, was less fortunate being severely damaged by an air–raid in 1940.[34]

Other candidates for preservation which were cut up in the enthusiasm for the munitions scrap drive are listed by Barker. These included ex–Isle of Wight Railway 2–4–0T *Ryde* and Dougal Drummond's personal 4–2–4T combined locomotive and inspection saloon nicknamed "The Bug". Both were cut up at Eastleigh works where they had been stored. Here also the small relics collection was dispersed and its paintshop home was converted to a gun shop for munitions work.[35] As there are indications that there were other unofficial collections of relics like that at Eastleigh at various railway workshops, one may only speculate as to how much other historical material was lost as Britain's railway industry directed its efforts to war work.

The grouping of railway companies in 1923 had a significant impact on the history of railway preservation in Britain; this coupled with the various centenary celebrations from 1925 onwards created a climate in which a sense of perspective in railway history was achieved. The public, especially those with an informed interest in railways, were able to exert some influence on the "Big Four" companies which found themselves in a far better position than the myriad of pre–grouping companies to review the historical significance of their assets and retain important examples. The most remarkable product of this was the LNER's York Railway Museum which showed what a sympathetic approach at the highest levels could achieve and gave an example which others unfortunately failed to follow.

Nevertheless there was within the railway industry an increasing recognition of the value of preserved items although on occasion their eventual fate was unclear. Because there was, in most cases, no clear policy on what should or should not be retained much depended on individual personalities: contrast for example the sympathetic approach of Gresley with that of Stanier. Changes in management or personnel could lead to the speedy destruction of items which had been carefully collected over a number of years. Despite the undoubted achievements during the inter–war period its most regrettable feature was temporary preservation which resulted in items being saved for a short time and then disposed of.

References

1. P Winding, *Preserving the Past, Part 1: The problems of selecting examples from Britain's 140 years of locomotive development*, Railway Magazine, 112, (1966), 553–7, p.555

2. W O Skeat, *Ruminations on Replicas*, Yesteryear Transport, 1, 2 (1972) 62–64 p.63

3. L T C Rolt, *The Railway Museum York*, (London, 1958), p.4

4. C J Allen, *One Hundred Years of Locomotives*, Railway World, 27 (1966) 170–175 p.174

5&6. Allen, p.175; *Liverpool & Manchester Centenary Celebrations*, Railway Magazine, 67, (1930), 353–365 p.355

7. A Jarvis and L Morris, *Lion,* (Liverpool, 1980)

8. Quoted in Jarvis and Morris, p.6

9. Jarvis and Morris, p.9

10. G Simpson, *Saving a Loco – 1927 Style*, Steam Railway, 1 (1981) pp.40–42

11. R Barker, *'Lost' Preserved Railway Rolling–Stock*, Transport History, 9, (1978) 100–109, p.103

12. J B Radford, *Derby Works & Midland Locomotives*, (London, 1971), p.188

13. J B Radford, *158A – The Story of a Veteran Locomotive*, The Wyvern, 1, 31 (1977) 8–9

14. E L Forge, *An Earlier Eastleigh Museum*, Railway Magazine, 131, (1985) 62–64

15. *The Preservation of Railway Relics*, Railway Magazine, 71, (1932), 219–221

16. Ibid, p.221

17. J Simmons, *Dandy–Cart to Diesel: The National Railway Museum* (London 1981), p.2

18&19. Rolt, p.3, North Eastern Railway Magazine, (1922) quoted in: K Hoole *The Railway Museum at York,* SLS, 51, (1975) 275–8, p.275

20. Rolt, pp.3–4

21. K Hoole, p.275

22. O S Nock, *Historical Steam Locomotives*, (London, 1959), p.60

23. *Through the York Museum*, Railway Wonders of the World, 1, (1935) 465–470, p.465

24. H C Casserley, *Railways Between the Wars*, (Newton Abbot, 1971) p.26

25. *The Preservation of Railway Relics*, Railway Magazine, 71, (1932), p.219

26. T Sheppard, *Collecting Museums,* Hull Museum Publication No. 184, (Hull 1935) no page numbers

27. T Sheppard, *Record of Additions*, Hull Museum Publication No. 181, (Hull, 1933) no page numbers

28. T Sheppard, *Catalogue of the Railway Museum, Paragon Station, Hull*, Hull Museum Publication No. 200, (Hull, 1938), p.1

29. H C Casserley, *Preserved Locomotives*, Fifth Edition, (London, 1980), p.35

30. J Bradshaw, Personal correspondence, 22 February 1984

31. Hoole, pp.276–277

32. Jarvis, Morris, p.10

33. Nock, pp.16–17

34. Barker, pp.103–104

35. Forge, p.64

10 The Great International Exhibitions - railway prizewinners and the National Railway Collection

Helen Ashby

It can be argued that the core of the National Railway Collection is its magnificent display of locomotives and rolling stock but the Collection is much richer and more comprehensive than these larger objects indicate. It reflects the whole history of Britain's railways and tells the story of technological evolution and of social change – the story of the people who created the railways, ran them, worked on them or travelled on them. In this capacity the National Railway Museum is home to an enormous range of objects from one of the largest locomotives ever built in Britain to the smallest uniform button, from a stately Royal Saloon to a humble workman's ticket.

Among this rich and varied material is the numismatics collection which in itself charts some of the major events in the story of the railways and helps illustrate their physical and social development. The collection consists of some 600 medals and medallions dating from the early 19th century and is still being added to today. A large proportion are commemorative medals which were struck to mark some important event or achievement and issued for sale or for general distribution. The issue of commemorative medals in Britain dates back to Tudor times when the medallic art was imported from the Continent. In the Victorian era and particularly during the Railway Mania, many medals were issued with a railway theme. Specially designed medals were often awarded in recognition of some outstanding achievement. Many of these were presented to individual railwaymen whilst others went to the railway companies which were business rivals and constantly striving to outpace their competitors.

Plate 10.1
Many railway companies printed elaborate catalogues of their exhibits which were distributed from the exhibition stands. Some of them, particularly from the Paris Exhibition of 1900, have survived in the National Railway Collection

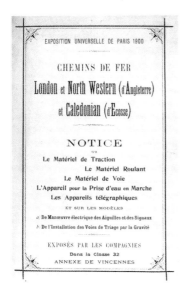

The development of the railways and the blossoming artistic tradition of the commemorative medal came at a time of great national and imperial pride. It was the age of the World's Fairs and the great International Exhibitions when Britain was eager to proclaim herself "Mistress of Invention". As the great technological invention of the day the railways played a significant part in these exhibitions and brought home many of the prizes, some of which took the form of elaborate medals inscribed with the name of the recipient. Many such medals have been preserved in the National Railway Collection and research in contemporary catalogues of the exhibitions also preserved at the Museum, establishes, in many cases, that the Collection also holds the original items for which the medal was awarded.

Perhaps the best known of the international exhibitions is the Great Exhibition of 1851, which was the "largest, most lavish and best attended display of accomplishments and projections into the future ever assembled". It was the brainchild of Prince Albert who devised an ambitious plan for a great international collection with the expressed purpose of "exhibition, competition

and encouragement", with prizes totalling over £20,000. It was based on four main categories – Raw Materials, Machinery and Mechanical Invention, Manufactures, and Sculpture and Plastic Art, all reflecting contemporary taste and innovation. Awards were presented to several railway companies for their exhibits including the London & North Western Railway 2–2–2 Express Passenger Locomotive No. 3020 *Cornwall*, built at Crewe in 1847, which is among the earliest surviving locomotives in the National Railway Collection.

The Great Western Railway Company exhibited its impressive 4–2–2 Broad Gauge locomotive *Lord of the Isles* in Hyde Park for the 1851 Exhibition and this same engine was subsequently the winner of an elegant bronze medal depicting Columbus discovering the Americas at the World's Columbian Exposition held in Chicago forty–two years later to commemorate the four hundredth anniversary of the landing of Columbus in October 1493.

Unfortunately the engine itself was scrapped in 1905 though some of the original components, including the fine brass nameplates were saved for the nation and are now displayed in the Great Western Railway Museum in Swindon along with the medal awarded at the Great Exhibition of 1851.

The Amsterdam Exhibition of 1895 saw the Midland Railway as a prizewinner receiving a more modest gilt alloy medallion depicting the Arms of Amsterdam on the obverse and on the reverse a delicate oak leaf design surrounded by a laurel wreath. The Company brought home a further award from the Brussels Exhibition of 1897. The Midland was not the only British prizewinner at Brussels that year since the Museum has four further examples of the medal awarded. Three of these medals are unprovenanced but the remaining example was awarded to the Great Western Railway Company for their fine display of views and posters.

Paris was the venue for major exhibitions in both 1889 and 1900 and British companies secured many prizes at both. In 1889 there were some 1,017 British exhibitors and 910 of these won awards in one or other of the five grades in which the recognitions were classified. Of these 43 were Diplomas of the Grand Prix, 218 were gold medals, 289 silver and 237 bronze medals, the remaining 123 were honourable mentions. *The Engineer* of 4 October 1889 lists the winners in the Industrial Section including a Grand Prix for the London & North Western Railway Company, gold and silver medals for the London Brighton & South Coast Railway Company, a silver for the London Chatham & Dover Railway Company, a Grand Prix for the Midland Railway Company, an Honourable Mention for the North London Railway and a gold medal for the South Eastern Railway.

A competition was held to find two different designs of bronze medal to be awarded to exhibitors. Fourteen designs were submitted to a jury. The entry selected for presentation to all exhibitors receiving awards was designed by Louis Bottee and depicts an allegorical scene showing France bestowing a laurel wreath on a male figure seated on his anvil above a panoramic view of the Eiffel Tower in the Champ de Mars where the exhibits were displayed. The reverse of this medal shows a winged horn blower seated on an oak branch and the female bust of France as can still be seen on French postage stamps and coins today. The class of the award made was not indicated on the medals but the distinction was made in the accompanying Diploma certificates none of which appear to have survived in the Collection. The second medal design by Daniel Dupuis, which was awarded to officials and other collaborators of the Exhibition, again has a classical flavour depicting a seated figure of France crowning a humble artisan and accompanied by a child representing the Spirit of the Light of Reason, and once again the background of the scene is the Eiffel Tower and the Champ de Mars. The reverse of this medal is quite plain with its simple bust of France.

The Museum has inherited the Bottee medal awarded to the London Brighton & South Coast Railway for William Stroudley's *Gladstone* Class 0–4–2 Locomotive No 189 *Edward Blount* and a second example awarded to the London Chatham & Dover Railway Company, though the details of the exhibit are not yet known. The Collection also has an example of the Dupuis medal but unfortunately there is no record of the recipient.

Plate 10.4
Two medals were designed for the
Paris Exhibition of 1889. They are
similar in style, depicting
allegorical scenes of France
bestowing the laurel wreath on
industry against a background of
the Eiffel Tower and the Champ
de Mars.

The 1900 Paris Exhibition saw several more medals going to British exhibitors
and in these cases it is possible to relate the details of the exhibits to the medals
through the British Official Catalogue of the exhibition held in the Museum's
Reference Library. The Great Eastern Railway had two stands at the Exhibition
and the Museum now holds two bronze medals awarded to the Company. The
main exhibit was their 4–4–0 Bogie Express Engine No 1900 *Claud Hamilton*
(numbered especially for the year of the Exhibition), which the British Catalogue
boasts "burns liquid fuel or coal at will". The Company's other stand displayed a
working model of the same locomotive (scale 1in = 1ft), a map and photographs
of the railway system and a model of the Royal Mail twin–screw steamer *Berlin*.
Unfortunately none of these items appear to have survived although the
National Collection does hold a fine contemporary model of "Claud Hamilton".

The North Eastern Railway won a pair of gold medals for their S Class 4–6–0
Express Passenger Locomotive No 2006, built at Gateshead Works in 1899,
designed for working the heavy East Coast Expresses between England and
Scotland.

One of the finest carriages in the National Railway Collection is the opulent
West Coast Joint Stock Dining Car No 76 which was built in 1900 and which
served exclusively as the Royal Dining Car on the West Coast Route between
1904 and 1956. The London & North Western and Caledonian Railways were
the proud winners of a bronze medal for this coach at the Paris Exhibition and
the medal has also found a permanent resting place in the Museum at York.

Plate 10.5
The sumptuous interior of the West Coast Joint Stock First Class Dining Car No. 76 which served in the Royal Train between 1904 and 1956 and is now preserved in the National Railway Collection

It is important to note that locomotives and rolling stock were not the railways' only forte but that their prowess was displayed and rewarded in the many and diverse fields which make up the railway business. The London & South Western Railway was among the prizewinners at the 1900 Exhibition, again with two medals having survived to reach the National Collection. Their exhibit was a model of the Southampton Docks and Harbour which was displayed in Class 29, covering models, plans and drawings related to Public Works.

The next International Exhibition represented in the National Railway Collection was the Louisiana Purchase Exhibition held in St Louis in 1904. The Collection contains four different classes of medal – bronze, silver, gold and the Grand Prize.

The bronze award is of particular interest since it is the first of these prize medals received by an individual rather than a Company. It is one of three medals won by one Joseph H Morton, who worked in the North Eastern Railway Headquarters in York, for his illustrated poster maps of the North Eastern System. Mr Morton went on to win prizes at the Franco–British Exhibition of 1908 and the Brussels Exhibition of 1910 and his medals were presented to the Museum by his niece in 1984. Unfortunately there is no evidence to suggest whether any of Mr Morton's maps have survived and certainly none have reached the National Collection.

The Brussels Exhibition of 1910 is particularly famous since the British section was destroyed by fire on 14 August of that year. Fortunately the prizes had already been awarded and though many of the items were lost in the blaze the medals still survive as testimony to their success. *Railway Magazine* of 1910 reported that no fewer than 58 locomotives were shown at the Exhibition and expressed its regret that no English firms were represented by Main Line Locomotive Engines.

The Great Western Railway however displayed a locomotive cab on which was installed their recently developed automatic audible signalling apparatus. The Company won a prize for the exhibit and the medal is preserved for posterity at the National Railway Museum.

Plate 10.8
Medals for the Brussels Exhibition of 1910 were struck in bronze, silver and gold, all in the same design. On the obverse Victory is seen bestowing a laurel wreath on a simple artisan against the majestic backdrop of the Grand Place in Brussels whilst the reverse depicts a horn blower mounted on horseback.

A fascinating record of some of the displays at the Brussels 1910 Exhibition preserved in the National Collection is a comprehensive catalogue of models owned by the London & North Western Railway Company and used by the Publicity Department for display at Exhibitions such as these. The Brussels exhibition saw the loss of many of these, all of which are carefully recorded in the catalogue as having been destroyed by fire, with an insurance claim noted of some £4,000. These exhibits included a model of the Liverpool & Manchester Railway Coach *Experience*, a ¼ in scale model of the West Coast Sleeping Saloon, a large model of the Edge Hill Gravitational Sidings at Liverpool, a model of electric points and signals, a model of the London & North Western Railway locomotive *Dreadnought*, another of the locomotive *Queen Empress*, one of the steamer *Hibernia*, a model of the steamer *Rathmore* and, more unfortunately, a stand carrying originals of Stephenson's letters which were also destroyed in the fire.

Other exhibits listed in that catalogue have survived and went on to be shown at many more exhibitions before finally coming to rest in the National Railway Museum. At the Japan–British Exhibition, White City, Shepherd's Bush in 1910 the London & North Western Railway Company exhibited Queen Adelaide's Saloon, a ¼ in scale model of King Edward VII's Saloon built at Wolverton Works and a small model of the Edge Hill Gravitational Sidings at Liverpool, all of which are now preserved. The Collection boasts one gold medal awarded at the exhibition, an unusually shaped creation depicting a globe supported by a Japanese Samurai Warrior and a British Knight in Armour. It was presented to a G Knight, but no record has yet been found of the winner or the exhibit.

A medal survives in the Collection from the International Exhibition at Ghent in 1913. This medal, designed by G Devreese, is in bronze and is rectangular in shape with one curved side. The obverse bears once again a traditional allegorical scene depicting a queen supported by Agriculture and Industry greeting three youthful nymphs. The reverse depicts two draped figures arranging flower garlands in a pavilion which represents the site of the Ghent Exhibition.

The Engineer of June 20th reports that the Ghent International Exhibition was a failure – "from the point of view of preparedness, of practical utility, of completeness and in the excitement of public interest". The special correspondent at Ghent suggests that this was largely due to bad management on behalf of the Belgian organizers but also reports that "it is becoming increasingly difficult to induce manufacturers of British machinery and supplies to expend money or time upon exhibits at foreign enterprises having for their avowed object the furtherance of international trade relations. The experience which has been theirs for the most part has not been such as to offer any great inducement to repeat the very serious outlay which they are called upon to bear...." It is certainly true that fewer railway companies visited this show and those that did took only stands of small exhibits, views, posters and plans. Exhibitors reported in *The Engineer* were the North Eastern Railway, Lancashire & Yorkshire Railway, Great Central Railway and the East Coast Joint Stock Committee.

The only exhibit reported on in Railway Magazine of 1913 was that sent by the Lancashire & Yorkshire Railway Company which included a selection of photographic views showing scenes from the Company's routes and models of the Company's steamers *SS Ouse* which worked the Goole and Continental Service, *TS Duke of Cumberland* which worked between Fleetwood and Belfast and *Colleen Bawn* from the Liverpool to Drogheda service. The model of *SS Ouse* has been preserved in the National Railway Collection and has been on loan to Hull City Museums for some years.

The final exhibitions from which medals have become part of the National Railway Collection are the British Empire Exhibitions held at Wembley in 1924 and 1925. The philosophy behind these exhibitions differed slightly from that of the earlier displays, with the threefold objective of displaying in the Motherland the resources of the Empire, indicating to its Dominions and Colonies the present state of the Motherland's productions, and above all of improving the acquaintance of each part with the others. *Engineering* of 31st October 1924 suggests that the Exhibition that year was a financial disaster since visitor figures fell far short of those expected owing to the "deplorable weather" that summer. However the true objectives of the Exhibition were deemed to have been fulfilled, a belief which is substantiated by the fact that the event was repeated the following year.

Plate 10.9
The medals created for the British Empire Exhibitions show a marked change in the design trend, moving away from the classical draped figures into a much more modern image. The 1924 medal depicts a simple stylised lion whilst the 1925 issue continues in the same style but reverts to the allegorical scene representing Agriculture, Art and Industry. Both medals share an identical reverse side with a crowned bust of the reigning monarch King George V.

At the 1924 British Empire Exhibition the London & North Eastern Railway was awarded a bronze medal for its display of "the First and the Last" – the first being *Locomotion No 1* which the Company inherited from the North Eastern Railway with the Grouping of the railways under the "Big Four" Companies in 1923. This locomotive hauled the first passenger train in the world on the Stockton & Darlington Railway in September 1825. It is now part of the National Railway Collection and can be seen on display at Darlington North Road Station Museum. The other half of the exhibit is not part of the National Collection but does still survive in working order. This is the London & North Eastern Railway's 4–6–2 Pacific locomotive No 4472 *Flying Scotsman* which was built at Doncaster in 1923 to the designs of Nigel Gresley, Chief Mechanical Engineer to the Company.

The following year at Wembley the London Midland & Scottish Railway won a medal and their stand featured once again the magnificent model of the West Coast Dining Car.

There were subsequent exhibitions but no significant railway company awards or exhibits have yet come to light. Two World Wars, the nationalisation of the railways and many other factors worked together to bring about great social and economic changes. Companies began to find that the cost of exhibiting, in terms of both time and money, outweighed the benefits since there was virtually no financial remuneration and little reward in terms of prestige or business gained. Now Britain is having to compete more strongly against foreign manufacturers and many of the great railway works of the late nineteenth and early twentieth centuries have closed. The Golden Age of the International Exhibition appears to have ended but a little of its spirit lives on in the rich legacy of prizes and exhibits preserved in the National Railway Collection.

References

The Art–Journal Illustrated Catalogue of the Industries of All Nations. *The Great Exhibition – London 1851*. Facsimile Reprint, David & Charles 1970

Railway Magazine, Vol 97 No 601 May 1951. *Railways and the Exhibitions of 1851 and 1951*. (299)

Railway Magazine, Vol 27 No 161 November 1910. *Railway Rolling Stock at the Brussels Exhibition*. (403)

Railway Magazine, Vol 33 No 3 September 1913. *The Lancashire & Yorkshire Railway and the Ghent International Exhibition*. (229)

North Eastern Railway Magazine, Vol 1 No 1 January 1911. *Interesting Exhibits at Brussels*. (21)

A Jacquet and E Tordeur, (1911) *Les Locomotives l'Exposition de Bruxelles 1910*. Revue Encyclopedique Belge des Chemins de Fer, Brussels

Administration des Chemins de Fer de l'Etat Belge (1913) *Notice sur l'Exposition Retrospective des Locomotives des Chemins de Fer de l'Etat Belge – l'Exposition de Gand (1913)*

London & North Eastern Railway (1925) *LNER Exhibit, Palace of Housing and Transport, Wembley 1925*

London & North Eastern Railway (1924) *The LNER Exhibit at the British Empire Exhibition, Wembley 1924*

Imprimerie Chaix (1900) *Exposition Universelle de Paris 1900, Chemins de Fer London et North Western (d'Angleterre) et Caledonian (d'Ecosse)*. Imprimerie Chaix, Paris

Offices of the Royal Commission (1900) Paris Exhibition 1900, British Official Catalogue. London & Paris

H J Campbell–Cornwall, (1968) *William Stroudley – Craftsman of Steam*. David & Charles, Newton Abbot

Engineering, Vol 47 (4 October 1889) *The Paris Exhibition Awards* (413)

Engineering, Vol 48 (26 July 1889) *Paris Exhibition Notes*. (116)

The Engineer, Vol 68 (4 October 1889) *Paris Exhibition, 1889 – British Section* (296)

The Engineer, Vol 115 (20 June 1913) *British Machinery at Ghent* (647)

Engineering, Vol 118 (31 October 1924) *Reflections on the British Empire Exhibition* (615)

11 An episode in railway publicity - tinplate advertising models of the Caledonian Railway

David Wright

The National Railway Museum holds a fine collection of models, ranging from the superb pairing, at 1:8 scale, of the Great Western Railway's 'King' class 4–6–0 express locomotive No. 6000 *King George V* and corridor composite 'Sunshine' brake coach No. 6484, built in the 1940s by B R Hunt of Johannesburg and exhibited for many years at Paddington Station, London, to the lilliputian 1950s home–assembly cardboard products of Micromodels Ltd, London EC4.

Towards the smaller–scale end, at gauge 0 (then 1"gauge) coarse scale, is found a distinctive pair of tinplate models, representing Caledonian Railway '903' class 4–6–0 locomotive No. 903 *Cardean* and West Coast Joint Stock corridor composite coach No. 384. Investigation shows that these models are survivors of an advertising campaign by the Caledonian Railway in 1908–9 of a type and scale probably unparalleled in railway history.

The years before the First World War were a time of intense competition between the railway companies and nowhere was this fiercer than in the battle for customers travelling from London to the North by way of either the East Coast Route (jointly operated by the Great Northern, North Eastern and North British Railway companies) or the West Coast Route (jointly operated by the London & North Western and Caledonian Railway companies).

The flamboyant General Manager of the Caledonian Railway, Guy Calthorp, was an enthusiastic advocate of advertising gimmicks as weapons in this campaign, and in December 1908, a 'small model Caledonian clockwork locomotive' had been released and 'although not an accurate model, it had a phenomenal sale'.[1] Details of this model do not appear to have survived; however, Calthorp was sufficiently encouraged by the response to this initiative to plan a much more ambitious project for 1909, executive responsibility being given to one of his assistants, Alex Fulton.

At this time the most prestigious service with which the Caledonian Railway was associated was the famous 'Corridor'– the 2pm express diner service between London (Euston) and Glasgow (Central) via the West Coast Route (Carlisle and Beattock, with a portion added or detached at Carstairs from or to Edinburgh) – then the heaviest regular express service in the country. The almost automatic choice of prototypes for publicity models were therefore No. 903 *Cardean* – the Caledonian locomotive in regular service on the 'Corridor' – in the case of a locomotive; and, for a coach, one of the impressive West Coast Joint Stock 12–wheelers, recently built especially for the 'Corridor' service.

The J F McIntosh–designed '903' class had been introduced in 1906, numbers 903–907 being put into traffic between May and July of that year. The first of the

Plate 11.1
Caledonian Railway 4–6–0 No. 903 *Cardean* preparing to leave Glasgow Central station with the 2pm 'Corridor' express diner service to Euston in 1908. Waiting at platform 3 with a local train is Caledonian Railway Brittain 2–4–0 No. 131, built in 1878.

class, *Cardean*, was named after the Perthshire estate of Edward Cox, a director of the company who later became deputy chairman, and it was soon put on the demanding 'Corridor' service. So suitable did it prove that it regularly hauled the service for the next ten years, achieving considerable fame: a reputation no doubt enhanced by the sleek, businesslike lines of the class and attractive Caledonian blue livery, despite which, alas, it was scrapped in 1930.[2]

Coach No. 384 was one of two West Coast Joint Stock corridor composites built at the London & North Western Railway's Wolverton Works in 1908 (Works drawing no. W22) for the Edinburgh portion of the 'Corridor', running between Carstairs and Edinburgh (Princes Street). At 65' 6" and weighing 42 tons, they were exceptionally luxurious and were right at the forefront of contemporary design practice. (Both 384 and the second coach, 383, were withdrawn in 1951).[3]

With these prototypes in mind, Alex Fulton approached Henry Greenly of Bassett–Lowke & Co, then the largest manufacturer of locomotive models in the country. After negotiation, an order for 30,000 each[4] of *both* coaches *and* locomotives was placed. Bassett–Lowke promptly subcontracted the production to Carette of Nuremburg in Germany and both coach and locomotive were produced in time for Christmas 1909, the coach appearing at the beginning of December and the locomotive during the middle of the month.

The prices were 1/6d (7½p) and 2/6d (12½p) respectively and the models were available at all Caledonian and London & North Western bookstalls. Although considered 'wonderful value'[5] at the time, they were not cheap when a weekly wage of about £1.10s (£1.50p) was the norm.

Plate 11.2
Tinplate model of Caledonian Railway No. 903 *Cardean* and West Coast Joint Stock corridor composite coach, made by George Carette of Nuremburg and supplied to the Caledonian Railway by Bassett - Lowke Ltd of Northampton

In contrast to many tinplate models of the period, these were remarkably true to prototype as the photographs show. Each model carried a discreet advertising panel, mounted so as not to detract from the general appearance: a transfer inside the tender of the locomotive and a small plaque under the coach body. Those who are familiar with the Scottish climate will appreciate the ambivalence of the wording on the latter!

The locomotive is equipped with a surprisingly powerful clockwork motor, with a fixed winding key projecting from the left–hand side of the 'firebox' between the rear pair of driving wheels. The driving wheels are authentically coupled and a thoughtful refinement is an automatic lock on the clockwork mechanism which is

Plate 11.3
Advertising panel in the tender of tinplate model of Caledonian Railway locomotive No. 903.

released when the locomotive is placed on a running surface. The finish and detail on both the locomotive and the coach are really quite impressive, although in fact the coach is mis–numbered '364', a number given to one of the 8–wheeled 45' 0" West Coast Joint Stock family saloons of 1899–1901.[6] The total length of the ensemble is 34" (see Plate 11.5). That Carette was the maker is evidenced by a very unobtrusive mark 'G.C.Co.N' (George Carette & Co Nuremburg) in red letters on the rear frame member of the locomotive below the cab: there is no maker's name on the coach.

However, at 4/– (20p) the pair, Calthorp could not have expected to make any money on the campaign – Carette's manufacturing costs and Bassett–Lowke's involvement must barely have been covered. Even had the vast stock been sold, any 'profit', as far as the Caledonian Railway was concerned, would have been indirect.

If the production figure really was 30,000 of each model, it follows that the investment in the campaign was in the region of £6000. To modern eyes this may appear a modest figure: but when it is considered that a new '903' class locomotive cost £3500,[7] that a third class single fare from London to Glasgow cost about £1.8s (£1.40), and that a pint of beer cost the equivalent of 1p, the true extent of the investment – indeed the risk – becomes apparent: something of the order of £750,000 at 1992 prices. And, at 4/–, economies were inevitable and the most obvious one is the non–articulation of the bogies on both locomotive and coach.

This may well have proved fatal to the success of the campaign. On the one hand, good value though they were by the standards of the time, they were large for models which could only run in a straight line. On the other, lacking bogies, they could not be used on a normal track layout: either of which shortcomings could

very well have dissuaded potential customers. Furthermore, the locomotive was only just available in time for Christmas and may have missed a proportion of its potential purchasers.

In any event, although figures are not available, 'sales were disappointing' and it seems very likely that most of the models were later scrapped. The fact is that Calthorp seriously overestimated his market and had over–ordered accordingly. It has been suggested[8] that his resignation from the Caledonian Railway in August 1910 could have been related to the failure of this project and the financial loss it incurred.

What is certain is that never again did the Caledonian Railway, or any other British railway company, produce advertising toys of this level of extravagance in comparable numbers.

After the War, other 'toys and pastimes' were produced under the aegis of the railway companies, of which the most successful were probably the range of jigsaw puzzles made for the Great Western Railway by the Chad Valley Co of Harborne and the 'Beautiful Britain' playing cards made for the London & North Eastern Railway by John Waddington Ltd of Leeds; but in these cases the errors of the Caledonian campaign were avoided by producing items appropriate to the travelling public but of wider appeal and utility, at low unit cost, with a profit margin for the railway company as well as the manufacturer. The few Caledonian tinplate models that survive serve as a reminder of an ambitious mistake, the lessons of which were learned by other railway companies.

References

1. *Model Railways*, November 1909, p.377
2. C P Atkins, (1976), *The Scottish 4–6–0 Classes*, Ian Allan Ltd, London, Chapter 5
3. D J Jenkinson, (1978), *An Illustrated History of LNWR Coaches*, Oxford Publishing Co, Oxford, Chapter 6
4. R Fuller, (1984), *The Bassett–Lowke Story*, New Cavendish Books, London, pp.28–29
5. *Model Railways*, December 1909, p.411
6. R M Casserley and P A Millard, (1980), *West Coast Joint Stock*, Historical Model Railway Society, Frome
7. H J C Cornwell (1974), *Forty Years of Caledonian Locomotives*, David & Charles, Newton Abbot, P.117
8. R Fuller, (1984) op. cit

12

Skegness is so Bracing

Beverley Cole

The *Jolly Fisherman* poster *Skegness is so Bracing* is arguably the most famous English railway poster and probably the most famous holiday poster ever drawn. It was first published in 1908 by the Great Northern Railway (GNR) which ran between King's Cross, Doncaster and Leeds and also extended to the small Lincolnshire coastal town of Skegness. The GNR paid twelve pounds for the "Masterpiece". Its greatness was not appreciated at the time as "real" artists were paid in guineas whilst commercial artists were not considered worthy of such prestige and only paid in pounds.

It was used to advertise excursions from London's King's Cross station to Skegness for a return fare of three shillings (15p today). The first trip took place on Good Friday, 1908, leaving King's Cross at 11.30 am. These excursions ran up to the August Bank Holiday of 1914 and the very last excursion from King's Cross to Skegness ran as late as 15th September 1984.

Plate 12.1
London & North Eastern Railway Poster: Skegness is so Bracing. 1926
(NRM Ref 75/38/32)

The *Jolly Fisherman* has been caricatured over and over again and re–drawn many times. Even at its time it was an exceptional poster, as most Edwardian and Victorian posters were restrained and factual. The *Jolly Fisherman* was an English alternative to Mucha's provocative mademoiselles. He is the epitome of good–clean–British–fun. His portly appearance and air of contentment imply affluence to appeal to the workman and his family. In more ways than one, the *Jolly Fisherman* was steadfastly pipe in the mouth!

The idea for the poster came from the myth of Romulus and Remus. The artist claimed that just as Remus leapt over the city wall of Rome, "Skegness is so glorious that it makes people jump without having anything to jump over".[1] The original design was incorporated into the Mayoral chain of office and now, ironically, welcomes car drivers to the town.

The artist of this famous poster was John Hassall who also has a fascinating life story. He was born in 1868 and died in 1948. His obituary in *The Times* on Tuesday 9 March 1948, described him as the "King of poster artists". He was born in Deal, Kent and after being educated at Worthing School and Newton Abbot College, he tried for a commission to Sandhurst. After twice failing to gain a place he emigrated to Manitoba, Canada, to join his brother. He later returned to England followed by studies in Antwerp and Paris. He started his own art school in the 1900s called "The New Art School and School of Poster Design". He married twice and was said to have had a tendency towards tall stories and drink. His daughter said "He would come back after two or three days of absence with a bruised face and no account of where he had been".[2]

One of his hobbies was to collect flints and random stones from the seashore. He eventually presented his collection of flints to Cambridge University. In his will he asked to be buried with his two favourite flints. John Hassall, like the *Jolly Fisherman*, was larger than life. The *Jolly Fisherman* could have been a cartoon caricature of himself. He too was heavily moustached and bald.

John Hassall spent most of his holidays in Walton–on–the–Naze, a genteel seaside resort near Clacton on the Great Eastern Railway, where he bought a cottage. He visited Skegness only once, in 1936, when he was presented with an illuminated address granting him "the freedom of the foreshore" by the Urban District of Skegness. He said "The reality of Skegness has eclipsed all my anticipations. It is even more bracing and attractive than I had been led to expect". When he died the Skegness corporation sent a wreath in the form of the *Jolly Fisherman*.

The original artwork for the poster now hangs in Skegness Town Hall. It was formally presented to the town by British Railways, along with the copyright, in 1966. Although this particular poster has become John Hassall's trademark it is only one example of his extraordinary talent and many of his other works deserve equal praise.

Railway posters were generally printed in two different sizes known as Double Royal which measured 40" x 25" and Quad Royal which measured 40"x 50". They were printed by the lithographic process. Although the National Railway Museum does not hold a copy of the Great Northern Railway version of the *Jolly*

Fisherman poster there are several other versions in the Collection. In Double Royal format, as the original, there is the London & North Eastern Railway 1930s version. This differs from the original in that the *Jolly Fisherman's* hands are pointing downwards rather than upwards, a pier has been added, some clouds removed and the whole image has been framed with a blue border. This has obviously been re–drawn. Other Double Royal posters were issued by British Railways around 50 years after the original. At this time a new character was introduced to join the *Jolly Fisherman* in the shape of a young boy wearing wellington boots, swimming trunks and a sou'wester and brandishing either a balloon or seaweed. One poster shows the boy running alongside the *Jolly Fisherman* past a funfair. The caption reads "Old and Young find Skegness is so Bracing". A second poster shows the young boy with the *Jolly Fisherman* in a vignette below him. Yet another poster shows a floodlit fair in which the *Jolly Fisherman* is again in a vignette and the *Skegness is so Bracing* slogan has been omitted.

Of the Quad Royal posters three were published by the London & North Eastern Railway. One is an elongated version of the Great Northern Railway poster, one advertising the Butlins Camp at Skegness built in 1937 with the *Jolly Fisherman* featuring in the bottom right–hand corner and the third by Frank Newbould after John Hassall showing the *Jolly Fisherman* being pulled by his scarf along the beach by a small girl. The National Railway Museum also has the artwork for this particular poster. The Quad Royal British Railways poster is of the Lincolnshire coast, again showing a vignette of the *Jolly Fisherman*. The National Railway Museum also has posters produced by the Skegness Advancement Association with an aerial view of Skegness and the *Jolly Fisherman* leaping towards the town.

The *Skegness is so Bracing* slogan is believed to have been the idea of Mr Hiley, the Chief Passenger Agent for the Great Northern Railway. At this time seaside towns were becoming popular and the working man could visit them for day trips during the summer. Skegness was conveniently accessible by rail from Nottingham and Leicester. Skegness advertised itself as a healthy seaside town. In 1897, a few years before the birth of the *Jolly Fisherman* poster, the *Great Northern Railway Seaside, Farmhouse and Country Lodgings Hotel Guide* described Skegness as a watering place: "Recently sprung into the front rank of health and holiday resorts ... with its long breezy promenade commanding the blue expanse of the German Ocean ... is comfortably reached by the Great Northern Line". It was then a rival to Cromer, Yarmouth and Margate with a population of 1,488 and recommended as a cure for "Sufferers from Phthisis (consumption), Bronchitis, Rheumatism and Kindred ailments".

Another work of art by John Hassall, bought by the National Railway Museum in October 1988 for £2,400, is appropriately entitled *The Skegness Cure* and was used in a newspaper advertisement and most probably as a poster as well, to publicise in 1911 and subsequently the same excursions from King's Cross to Skegness that had been promoted by the original *Jolly Fisherman*. The painting shows what could be the *Jolly Fisherman* in his Sunday best pulling an invalid along the beach at Skegness. Yet another similar design is that of *Grandma Skegness* – a Mother Twankey type figure bouncing along the beach in her long summer frock and festooned in a flowery hat with ribbons serving as a wind

Plate 12.2
Great Northern Railway : original
artwork for the poster "Skegness
Cure". 1911
(*NRM Ref 88/22/41*)

blown scarf. This was published some years after the *Jolly Fisherman* poster and
was never as popular.

The *Jolly Fisherman* is still promoting Skegness as the ideal holiday resort: 1988
was his eightieth birthday. A special excursion train was chartered from King's
Cross to Skegness and the passengers were charged the original ticket price and
wore period costume. Throughout the year there were exhibitions and parties to
celebrate his birth.

Today *The Jolly*, as the Skegness publicity department refer to him, can be seen
around Skegness at the theatre, children's parties and on the foreshore shaking
visitors' hands. He is not one person, however, but the whole publicity
department, including the female members of staff who appear in the costume of
white trousers, blue jumper, black scarf and black wellingtons when the occasion
arises. There are two sculptures of him in Skegness. One can be seen in the

Compass Gardens which was sculpted by Ron Walker of Skipton and the other was commissioned by David Perry of British Rail's Community Unit and erected in Skegness station in May 1989.

It does seem that John Hassall's *Jolly Fisherman* is immortal, unlike the artist who died in relative obscurity in 1948. However, Hassall's spirit of enterprise, energy, sense of humour and love of English life live on in the *Jolly Fisherman* poster.

References

1. J T Shackleton, *The Golden Age of the Railway Poster*, New English Library, 1976, p.46
2. Bevis Hillier, *Posters*, Spring Books, 1969

This article was first published in *The Friends of the National Railway Museum Newsletter*, No. 50, 1990, pp.14–16

13 The Curator's dilemma in operating railway artefacts

Richard Gibbon

Curators in technical museums have long faced the dilemma that, in choosing to operate items for which they are responsible, they ultimately destroy the integrity of that object – at least at the time it came into their care. In a paper published in 1981, David M Baird justifies the operation of railway rolling stock "in regular use and well maintained" by dismissing criticism of continual renewal of components.[1] He argues that the artefact is only a collection of pieces that have coincidentally arrived together as a result of previous components wearing out and being replaced during a lifetime of service. He quotes the adage of George Washington's axe with its twenty–six new heads and forty–five new handles. His argument deserves further analysis, however, because the paper is used to support the main–line running programme for Canadian Pacific steam locomotive No. 1201 which is apparently a railway enthusiast's dream. Its custodians expect to be able to keep it running for the next hundred years.[2] This is contrasted with static locomotives stored out of doors on plinths which are said to need to be written off over the next 25 years.[3] In either case both objects will have been totally transformed from their original form – in museum terms – at the end of their respective periods of operation or display.

This paper seeks to examine the influences that bring about changes being made to components that wear out or degrade and to discuss from a curatorial viewpoint the best way of managing or resisting these changes where appropriate. Museum objects in the National Railway Collection may vary from fine china and silver to full–size pieces of rolling stock. It is with the latter – and particularly locomotives – that this paper is mainly concerned but the general principles outlined below have, to a greater or lesser degree, almost universal application.

Construction materials used for the building of railway rolling stock are almost always "biodegradable". Baird in his paper on "Storage and Use of Railway Equipment"[4] illustrates well the view that rolling stock is inexorably deteriorating and storage in the care of museums must be more active than the all too common practice of leaving the vehicle outdoors on a siding until resources allow the conservation/restoration programme (if one exists) to start work on it.

Indeed, it is interesting to note that the quality of the storage afforded to vehicles is often affected by the perceived attractiveness of the object as well as its physical condition.

At the National Railway Museum locomotives and Royal Coaches are invariably kept under cover in a relatively controlled environment and freight vehicles are nearly always stored out of doors. It could be argued, however, that an elderly locomotive if properly prepared can survive outside without sustaining damage better than an elderly wooden freight vehicle, which even if protected from direct ingress of water will suffer from damp and frost damage. The changes that occur during the life of an object taken into museum care, are of great interest and must be of consequent concern to curators. The situation is made more difficult because objects usually find their way to a museum near the end of their useful working lives and significant inherent changes may already be well under way. What follows explores those changes and discusses their importance in relation to their effect on the well being of the object. Particular attention is drawn to the consequences of a decision to operate certain objects in revenue earning service on the mainline railway or on a preserved line.

Six categories of change are discussed.

1. Changes that are made during the working life of the object causing variations from the manufactured item, up to the point at which it was placed in the care of the museum.

2. Changes that are made to enable the object to be restored to fit condition to run safely and effectively on the main–line railway.

3. Changes that are made to "improve" the performance of the object once it has been restored to running condition.

4. Changes that are made to create a deliberate effect which enhances the way in which the object "works" for the Museum.

5. Changes that are made to re–create a previous form of the object not represented by its condition at withdrawal from service.

6. Changes that are made to prevent deterioration of the object and to stabilize its condition.

These changes can cause the dilemmas which are the subject of endless debate and which cause a polarization of professional views.[5] It is the curator's role to use judgement so that during the period the museum is taking care of the object its long term future is not jeopardized. Many of the changes outlined above are totally reversible and leave the integrity of the object intact but others, which mostly fall into category 2, are irreversible and are typically of the same type of change as category 1, ie replacement of worn–out parts such as occurred during the object's working life. These in particular are the changes that create difficulties and must not be undertaken lightly without first considering the implications for the long term future of the object.

1. Changes made during the working life

The object that the Museum acquires is likely to be quite different from the brand–new item that originally entered service. This is well illustrated by the fact that *Mallard* is not now the same collection of components that achieved a speed of 126 mph in 1938.[6] The London Midland & Scottish Railway had a technique in its Crewe workshops that involved the locomotives coming in for heavy repair, being stripped right down to suitable collections of parts which were sent away to their respective departments for overhaul/replacement.[7] Refurbished collections of parts (not necessarily the same ones) returned to the erecting shop and were re–assembled onto a spare set of frames. This was done because the frames were the last component to be freed by stripping and were the first component required for re–erection. Any necessary mechanical work on the frames could entail delays in the throughput of repaired locomotives. The spare set enabled the locomotives to emerge rapidly from a heavy repair. This meant that the only original parts of the locomotive that were guaranteed to re–appear on the appropriately numbered rebuilt locomotive would be the motion and nameplates.

The above illustration serves to show that even if the design of the object was never substantially altered during the working life (as with the Merchant Navy Pacifics of O V S Bulleid) the collection of components may not be what it seems. The high standard of paintwork and exhibition finish applied to the locomotive in the Museum's care only serves to strengthen the view that the original machine "as built" has survived intact. Detailed examination of much of the Museum's rolling stock collection will show that many items change as a matter of routine. It will come as no surprise therefore to learn that *Duchess of Hamilton* 46229 is equipped with driving wheel axleboxes from sister locomotive, 46209.

Whilst the Crewe example is not wholly typical it is inevitable that major overhauls and rebuilding will cause the integrity of the collection of parts to be questioned. All we can say with certainty is that a particular object represents the condition of the object as acquired by the Museum. What is important from that point onwards is that deterioration or alteration is controlled sensitively. The pedigree of the collection may not be perfect for some objects but the curator must never be allowed to assist in the destruction of what is left.

2. Changes to fit the vehicle for main line running

There are a number of examples of recent major changes on British preserved locomotives:

> Replacement of flawed driving axle detected as faulty during ultrasonic examination, 60009 *Union of South Africa*

> Reboring of cylinders and piston valve bores with attendant replacement of piston and valve heads, 4771 *Green Arrow*

> Replacement of boiler components, eg steampipe, lap seams, tubes, 46229 *Duchess of Hamilton*

Wheel or tyre replacement/turning, 6023 *King Edward II*

Tender tank redesign to alter coal/water ratio to more favourable value: 46229 *Duchess of Hamilton*

Lowering overall height of locomotive, 46229 *Duchess of Hamilton*

This last item was carried out during the major refit of the *Duchess of Hamilton* locomotive to work on the British Railway network where the presence of 25Kv over–head electric wires led to the prohibition of any vehicle with an overall height exceeding 13ft 1in. This prohibition was brought in when the locomotive was in the final year of a 5–year rebuilding programme and the Museum was left with little alternative but to rebuild the cab. This task, however, brought its own rewards by a curious quirk of fate. When the front plates of the cab (which had remained unmodified throughout the life of the locomotive) were rubbed down before painting, the profile of the joint with the previous streamlined casing was revealed. The casing was carried only until 1945 and this indentation provided the only remaining physical (non–photographic) evidence of the locomotive's streamlined career.

Care must be taken to ensure that the demands of running on the main–line for an object as emotive as a steam locomotive, are not so strong as to cloud the issue of curatorial integrity. The problem is exacerbated by the need for full power performance. Although the Museum is represented on the footplate at all times, working on heavy gradients the loading and the length of climb determine that the power outputs required to keep to time may be close to the design power of the locomotive when built fifty or so years ago. Therefore unlike entering veteran cars in the London to Brighton road–run where care and consideration for the elderly mechanism can result in "soft pedalling", the only way to complete the rail journey is to drive the machine as it was built to be driven. The analogy with historic aircraft which fly at displays is most apt. To take off with such machines, full power has to be developed and there is no place for the faint hearted in such an operation. Unhappily the consequences of component failure with historic aircraft are dire as witnessed by the total destruction of the only surviving Bristol Bulldog in 1964[8] and the only surviving Bristol Blenheim in 1987[9] Both were fully restored machines doing the job they were built to do originally. Inevitably we must question the risks involved in such operations.

3. Changes to improve performance

At first this would appear to be a dangerous category for museum involvement. For example the type of work undertaken to improve the draughting of BR No. 71000 *Duke of Gloucester* shows that the locomotive was not developed to its full power potential during its working life and that subsequent modifications have no doubt increased power output. This work would fall outside the remit of the National Railway Museum but adds to the historical aspects of a locomotive in which the Museum has an interest. However, more subtle changes have taken place since the demise of steam on BR which need careful consideration.

Modern lubricants for example, with improved lubricating properties are now available and many of the older types of "straight" additive–free oils are difficult to obtain. The oil companies are anxious to assure museum users that their modern product is in every way equivalent to the original product but their data–sheets do not concern themselves with one physical property which, though irrelevant to modern day lubricants, is vital to our own application. That is the ability of the oil to "wick" or to draw itself up a worsted woollen trimming and feed freely over the bearing surfaces by the use of capillary attraction. The Museum workshops must confirm that the oils used on rolling stock have equivalent or better wicking characteristics before a change is approved. In a similar vein the use of PTFE in gland packings in place of graphited yarn/asbestos has extended the time between repacking valve spindles and enhanced the performance of the gland assembly. The fact that these changes are reversible helps greatly in assessing the way forward.

A further example of "legitimate" modification to improve performance concerns the design of the replacement superheater elements for use in the *Duchess of Hamilton's* boiler. In this case the performance in question is not that of the locomotive but the performance of the engineering component as a successful part of a preserved and operating locomotive.

When steam locomotives were in service every day of the week they seldom cooled down and unlike the Museum's operating locomotives – which spend long periods between runs stored cold – their boilers and superheaters were warm for most of the time and prevented the accumulation of condensation which lies in the horizontal sections of the superheater elements unable to drain away. Over a long period the water gradually evaporates at room temperature leaving behind carbonic acid of increasing concentration as time goes on. This acid will form small cavities in the lower side of the steel superheater pipes and lead to drastic failure (Plate 13.1). The design of the elements is such that the only way to remove the water during a stored period is to extract the superheaters from the boiler and stand them up vertically to drain and ventilate.[10] This is a labour intensive job which furthermore destroys the integrity of the previously examined and certified steam line. Superheater elements are expendable items like boiler tubes and in service would have been replaced on a regular basis. In securing new elements it has proved difficult to obtain the trifurcated joint which was used to split the steam line into three before it passed down the pipes. This was a specialist railway component which is not easily reproducible, (Plate 13.2). The replacement component made slightly differently is shown in (Plate 13.3) whereby the down comer on both input and outlet legs is lengthened and three separate tee joints are created. Simply by putting a threaded drain plug into the thickened underside of each down comer pipe it is possible to drain the whole superheater during storage periods and allow the internal surfaces to dry out completely. This system is currently on trial at the National Railway Museum with the full approval of the mechanical and boiler inspectors of British Rail.

4. Changes to the way the object "works" for the Museum

These changes can be reversible or otherwise. Perhaps the most notable irreversible change is the sectioning of the rebuilt Merchant Navy locomotive *Ellerman Lines*.

Plate 13.1

Plate 13.2

Plate 13.3

The sectioning of technical artefacts is dealt with by Mann[11] and he concludes that the ideal way to address the problem of apparent destruction of the artefact is to acquire two identical objects. Since there are several complete Merchant Navy class locomotives in private preservation the Museum can justify the irreversible damage done since the value of the sectioned locomotive as a teaching aid and as a visually exciting object is unquestioned.

The change of identity of A4 locomotives seems to be a particular favourite in the preservation world and indeed the Museum played host to the transformed *Bittern* which took on the guise of *Silver Link* in 1988. The change was confined to the cosmetic finish of the locomotive but was spectacular in its execution. The curatorial danger here is that visitors who are not fully informed will believe that the real locomotive survives and misinformation is spread.

In the last twelve months the A4 60009 has been seen as *Osprey, Union of South Africa* and even *Merlin* for a short period.[12] This makes newsworthy copy for magazines and excitement for photographers and enthusiasts, but it needs to be controlled to avoid confusion for the general public.

5. Changes made to recreate a previous form of the object

In this category come alterations necessary to put an object into a time period which reflects a condition other than that of its withdrawal from railway service. These changes invariably involve compromise because progress and development have taken place on the railway and the vehicle has been brought up to date according to current thinking. For instance the Southern Railway locomotives *Cheltenham* and *Sir Lamiel* should both be fitted with prominent snifting valves behind the chimney, if the livery they are displayed in is to be factually correct. The valves were removed at rebuilding. Similarly, the class 20 Diesel–electric locomotive is displayed in its 1957 form but still retains the later "Oleo" buffers that were fitted later in its life.

Generally such anomalies are technical but should be noted as significant variations to the material displayed rather than historical errors. Any such anomalies are invariably spotted quickly by knowledgeable visitors and the Museum should be well prepared for their observations.

6. Changes to prevent deterioration of the object

These changes are more subtle than the above matters and constitute much of the hard work behind the scenes in museums. The changes can be as simple as providing waterproof accommodation for wooden vehicles that are taking in water, or as complex as the process of chemical water treatment for the protection of the internal surfaces of a steam boiler. These actions generally are seen as an investment in the object's future and are perhaps the most important changes with which we are dealing.

With essentially static objects like the original *Rocket* and the Bury built Furness

Railway locomotive great care must be taken because of the physical frailty of the object and changes here can include treating wood and metal with rot inhibitors and taking the weight off elderly springs with carefully concealed props. There is, however, another aspect to this group of changes which relates directly to those vehicles running in service either regularly or intermittently. This involves the discipline that is to be used throughout the preparation, running and disposal of locomotives. Care taken here can prolong almost indefinitely the "non renewed" parts of the object. In this category would be the use of boiler feedwater treatment, regular underside cleaning and correct laying up procedures. Smokeboxes, fireboxes and ashpans should be swept and oiled after use; motion parts oiled and greased;boilers and tender tanks drained and well ventilated; cylinders should be given a plentiful supply of lubrication which is thoroughly circulated and oil film lubricated bearings should be moved regularly to keep squeezed–out oil films established. This also applies to internal combustion engines where cylinders and poppet valves can dry out and stick if left static for too long.

The comments relating to lubrication of bearings have a special relevance at the National Railway Museum where the establishment of a temporary exhibition in Swindon in the 1990 involved the movement of 40 vehicles by road and rail. Many of these vehicles had hardly turned a wheel in the preceding ten years and it was realised early on in the preparation process that the act of removing the vehicle from display to the workshops for examination was putting dried out journal bearings at risk. In order to avoid damage, vehicles were jacked up and a fresh oil film was established between journal, bearing and lubricating pad before the wheels were allowed to turn for the first time.

None of these tasks give the object infinite life but they will if carried out thoroughly mean that the degradation occurring through running a locomotive for example is minimal and perhaps occurs less rapidly than if the locomotive were on static display.

There are certainly many examples where specific components will last longer in intermittent use, than out of use. These include lead acid batteries, correctly lubricated journal bearings, rolling contact bearings, heavy current electrical machinery, crane/haulage wire ropes and brake cylinders.

Conclusions

The changes and modifications that are necessary to allow an item of rolling stock to run must be carefully considered in the light of the historic nature of the object. It must be borne in mind that the object, once restored to run, is at potentially far greater risk of damage, than when it is on display slowly degrading.

Replicas provide an excellent way round the problem of demonstrating ancient machines and attempts to resuscitate elderly locomotives in the collection should be resisted. The mechanical aspects of 'modern' locomotives should be kept in good condition, so that potential special occasion operation can be considered under controlled conditions.

Main line running of locomotives can be justified by showing that the benefits accrued from the extra care and attention lavished on the locomotive more than offsets the controlled wear on components which would normally be replaced on a regular basis anyway.

References

1 D M Baird (1981) *Storage and Use of Railway Equipment*, IATM VII 1981 p.43–62
2 D M Baird (1981) *Storage and Use of Railway Equipment*, IATM VII 1981 p.61
3 D M Baird (1981) *Storage and Use of Railway Equipment*, IATM VII 1981 p.48
4 D M Baird (1981) *Storage and Use of Railway Equipment*, IATM VII 1981 p.43–62
5 P R Mann (1989) International Journal of Museum Management and Curatorship, 8, p.369–387
6 Rutherford, M (1988) *Mallard The Record Breaker* p.29
7 Railway Observer 1959 Dec, Vol 29, No. 370, p.361
8 Flight International 1964 Sep p.505
9 Aeroplane Monthly 1987 August
10 Mid–Hants Railway Observed Procedure
11 P R Mann (1989) International Journal of Museum Management and Curatorship, 8, p.369–387
12 Steam Railway 1991 October and Railway World 1990 March

14 The National Railway Museum, York

Neil Cossons

This chapter was first published in 1976, as a critique of the National Railway Museum shortly after its opening in 1975. Its author little thought then that he would ultimately himself become Director of the National Museum of Science & Industry, and thus directly responsible for the future of the NRM. It is included in the present collection as a clear reminder of the NRM in the early days of John Coiley's reign. It has deliberately not been updated in any way, and this must be borne in mind in reading the text.

The steam railway, the first form of transport with which the mass of the populace had any contact, has captured the imagination of people throughout its existence. In the country of origin of the locomotive the opening of a new railway line was almost always an occasion for festivities and rejoicing; a century or more later the demise of steam on British Railways in the late 1960s evoked a wave of nostalgia quite without precedent. Today about a thousand steam railway locomotives are preserved in Britain, in museums, on privately–owned branch lines, or simply on short stretches of track where they can be put into steam for a few hours at a weekend. It is inevitable therefore that in the new National Railway Museum at York, Britain's first national museum to be devoted specifically to the celebration of a national achievement, the steam locomotive should play a dominant role. But this newest national museum is very much more than merely a railway enthusiast's paradise and it is this which sets it apart from many others of its kind, establishes its stature and importance and places it, rightfully, amongst the major historical and technological museums of the world. Here, for the first time a conscious attempt has been made to set the railway as a mode of transport in its historical context, to interpret its significance, explain its technology and illustrate its social and economic impact.

The National Railway Museum results directly from the 1968 Transport Act which established that the British Railways Board (BRB) should pass responsibility for its railway historical relics to the Department of Education and Science (DES), which in this context means the Science Museum. Furthermore the BRB would find and provide, in consultation with the Science Museum, a suitable site and building for the new museum. The prehistory of the railway museum however, is a long one of which coincidentally one of the earliest chapters opened in York itself. Here, in 1928, the London & North Eastern Railway set up the first York railway museum containing in the main locomotives, rolling stock and many small exhibits associated with railways in the North East of England. The only major anachronism in the collection was the London, Brighton & South Coast Railway 0–4–2 locomotive *Gladstone* obtained from the Southern Railway by the Stephenson Locomotive Society in 1927 and the first locomotive to be preserved by a society as distinct from a railway company. Thereafter museum preservation and society preservation pursued generally different tracks.

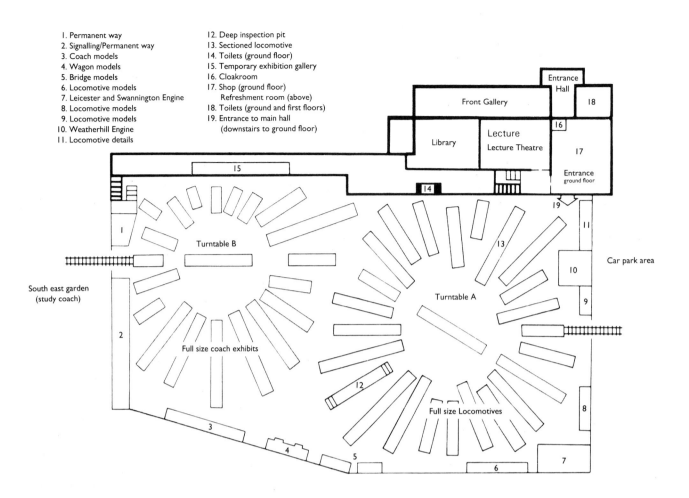

1. Permanent way
2. Signalling/Permanent way
3. Coach models
4. Wagon models
5. Bridge models
6. Locomotive models
7. Leicester and Swannington Engine
8. Locomotive models
9. Locomotive models
10. Weatherhill Engine
11. Locomotive details
12. Deep inspection pit
13. Sectioned locomotive
14. Toilets (ground floor)
15. Temporary exhibition gallery
16. Cloakroom
17. Shop (ground floor)
    Refreshment room (above)
18. Toilets (ground and first floors)
19. Entrance to main hall
    (downstairs to ground floor)

Figure 14.1

Ground plan of the original two-acre Main Exhibition Hall at the National Railway Museum, York (*NRM*)

Shortly after the nationalization of railways in 1948 the then British Transport Commission produced a report, published in 1951, in which it recognized the need to preserve the relics and records inherited from the old companies and the principle that their custody 'should be founded on a clear appreciation of the wider social and cultural heritage of early transport development in many fields'.[1] Significantly, it also indicated that the operation should be a continuing one, involving 'the gradual bringing up to date of the collection from internal sources'.[2] A Consultative Panel on Historical Relics was set up, a curator appointed and then began the formidable task of building up a representative national collection relating to the history of railways and canals. In addition to the then existing railway museum at York the report recommended that three others should be established, one in or near London, a second in Edinburgh and ultimately a third, to be in Cardiff. The actual results turned out somewhat differently. The Museum of British Transport was opened in a modified London Transport garage in 1961, whilst instead of Cardiff the Great Western Railway Museum was set up, jointly with the Borough Council, in a converted Methodist chapel in Swindon. In Scotland no specific national transport museum was built as moves to establish a transport museum under Glasgow Corporation ownership were already under way. Ultimately this museum inherited the Scottish locomotives scheduled by the BTC for preservation. Another museum which evolved from the same basic concept, although a completely separate set of initiatives, was the Waterways Museum at Stoke Bruerne, now operated by British Waterways Board.

By the late 1960s British Railways, in a state of post–Beeching shock and under a mandate to run at a profit, no longer found the high–minded ideals of 1951 acceptable and in the Bill which resulted in the Transport Act of 1968 the intention was announced to transfer the historical relics to the DES. The apprehension felt by many people about the future of the BRB relics and archives became particularly obvious in the debate of 8th October 1968 on the Transport Bill in the House of Lords, the first time there had been discussion of the clause because the guillotine procedure had prevented consideration by the Commons. Lord Hughes, speaking on behalf of the government, said: "There was a wide range of disagreement on what the Government proposed, the objection to transferring the records and relics, the fear that the methods proposed would lead to the break up of a collection and perhaps to the needless dispersal and even destruction of many relics which ought not to be dispersed or destroyed". He went on to say the "the decision to move to York is not a firm one ..... In the course of the considerations others may emerge to make York not the most suitable site". This was in response to considerable pressure to rehouse the Clapham collection in St Pancras which at that date was thought to have a limited life as a railway station. Miss Jennie Lee, Secretary of State for Education and Science, was quite categorical however when questioned on 5th December and in the course of her reply stated that a great deal of thought had been given to the possibilities of retaining a transport collection in London. "There was a belief that St Pancras or some other buildings in London were available; that is not so .... It is considered, since the Railways Board is decanting this into our Ministry, that to have one really first class museum at York is in the best interests of the people generally, and it is in keeping with Government policy that we should have some high points of excellence outside London as well as inside".

It was eventually decided to refurbish and extend part of the old York North Motive Power Depot for rehousing of the railway exhibits from the York Queen Street and Clapham museums together with certain items from the national collection which were still in store. The London Transport collection of trams and buses, also in the Clapham Museum, would not go to York and has subsequently been found a new home at Syon Park. Work began on the York buildings early in 1973 and on 27 September 1975, 150 years to the day after the opening of the Stockton & Darlington Railway, the first public railway in the world to operate both passenger and goods traffic by means of locomotives, HRH The Duke of Edinburgh declared open the National Railway Museum at York.

The larger part of the museum consists of the old motive power depot to which has been added a new building containing workshops, library, lecture theatre, refreshment room and offices. There are also two outside display areas. The Main Exhibition Hall, covering two acres, has forty–four railway tracks radiating from the two original turntables which have been retained and around which the locomotives and rolling stock are displayed. An important feature of the new museum is the direct rail connection to British Railways, something which Clapham lacked and from which it always suffered. This relative ease of exchanging stock by rail clearly has important implications for the way in which the Museum will develop and already the opportunity is being taken for adding new items as they become available and loaning out others. A high proportion of the national railway collection's large exhibits are in fact outside York and will always be so; on loan to other museums, running on preserved branch lines, or in

storage. Thus the museum is becoming the focal point of a much wider preservation movement in which certain locomotives and stock can be operated under properly controlled conditions all over the country. The selective relaxation by British Railways of the embargo on preserved locomotives running on its lines and the close relations which exist between museum and railway staff and private preservation organizations are all of benefit to the museum and will help to allay the frequent, if somewhat naive, criticisms made of all transport museums that they are dead.

From the outside the building is rather disappointing and despite the obvious constraints imposed by a restricted site British Railways' architects' department have missed any opportunity to let the function of the building express itself externally. The extensive use of grey brick, not only for the new additions to the building but also for cladding the whole exterior of the old depot contributes to this nondescript appearance. The poor condition of the old depot's original brickwork obviously needed some form of treatment; what is unfortunate is that the anonymity which has been created masks the vitality and colour of the museum's contents, but more particularly it fails to establish any feeling of permanence appropriate to the nature of the exhibits themselves.

Once inside the museum, however, any minor shortcomings in the external appearance of the building diminish to insignificance before the quality, quantity and tremendous emotive impact of the major exhibits in the Main Exhibition Hall which leads directly off the entrance area. The locomotives are clearly in their natural environment and look well in it. The retention of the 'A' turntable with its open pit contributes to this feeling of authenticity and in addition provides an admirable 'centre piece' display setting in which to place a choice exhibit. Immediately inside the Main Hall is a new addition to the collection which fills a long felt need in a British railway museum, a fully sectioned locomotive; in this case a rebuilt Merchant Navy Pacific, *Ellerman Lines*, raised slightly from the track and electrically powered to show the working of the motion. Some eleven tons of steel have been removed from the right–hand side of the locomotive and tender revealing the interior of the firebox with its unusual thermic siphons, the boiler and superheater tubes, smokebox and one cylinder and steam chest. Curiously, this technique has been successfully applied in a number of overseas railway museums but never done before in Britain. Its effectiveness in explaining the working of the steam locomotive is considerable. Adjacent to *Ellerman Lines* is the Weatherhill winding engine of 1833 used on the Stanhope & Tyne Railway until 1918 for hauling wagons and subsequently reassembled in the old Queen Street Museum. With the greater space available in the National Railway Museum the engine has been restored to working condition, complete with a new flywheel and is demonstrated from time to time using electric power. The Weatherhill engine, together with the Swannington incline winding engine from Leicestershire, both emphasize the significance of the stationary engine in the development of the steam railway and its role in the transitional stage between the horse as the primary form of motive power and the steam locomotive.

Plate 14.2
Carriages around 'B' turntable.
(NRM)

Surrounding 'A' turntable is the main part of the locomotive collection ranging in date from *Agenoria* of 1829 to *Evening Star*, the last locomotive to be built by British Railways, in 1960. The overwhelming atmosphere created by the locomotives at present on display is of the late Victorian and early Edwardian period, the golden age of the railway and no less than twelve of the locomotives in the gallery date from the period 1892 to 1905. There is an active policy, however, to broaden the base of the collection and to add diesel–hydraulic and diesel–electric locomotives to the electric engine already there. A recent addition, furthering the trend in this direction, is a vehicle from the experimental Advanced Passenger Train displayed to show the unique suspension system. Information on the large exhibits is provided on caption panels on which technical and non–technical data is clearly presented. Some of this data is also available in publication form. There is also a specially deepened and illuminated inspection pit to which visitors have access in order to view the underside of the locomotive on it.

The 'B' turntable at the other end of the Main Hall is the focal point of the display of passenger and goods stock although some items, including the BR Mark 1 coach used to accommodate school parties doing project work or eating packed lunches, are normally kept outside. The rolling stock collection is spectacular but by no means representative, including several specialized vehicles and three royal saloons. Nevertheless, there is an ordinary Midland Railway six wheel composite carriage of 1885, beautifully restored by British Rail Engineering Limited, at Wolverton and a Great Northern passenger brake of 1887. The same problem of scope applies in the case of goods vehicles of which there are very few, but there are plans to add more typical examples in the future. In this connection the museum has important and indeed vital power to its elbow in that it has inherited from the BRB museum the right to schedule items for preservation in advance of their withdrawal from service. These items are provided by BR at no purchase cost to the museum thus enabling it to operate a sensitive and systematic collecting policy.

Although the Main Hall is dominated by locomotives and rolling stock there are also displays around its walls devoted to various technical features of locomotives, passenger and goods vehicles together with bridges, permanent way and signalling. There is a comprehensive display of locomotive models covering a number of aspects not dealt with by full size exhibits. Of particular significance in this context is the British private locomotive building industry, of which most of the output went overseas. Overlooking this area is a balcony running along the west side of the Main Hall which besides affording a magnificent viewpoint from which to look down on the major exhibits, contains a gallery devoted to the history of railways, their growth, social and economic importance. This gallery is a highly successful combination of smaller exhibits and well presented information contained in captions, drawings, models and animations. A simple but very effective two–level caption system provides a non–technical narrative flowing through the display together with more detailed labels for individual exhibits.

On the right of the main entrance is the front gallery devoted to the display of railway paintings, glass, china and silverware, the full significance of which in art and design terms could well be developed further. Beneath the balcony is a temporary exhibition gallery. Another feature of this section of the museum is the 80–seat lecture theatre which forms the focal point for much of the museum's educational activities. Lectures and demonstrations are presented here on a regular basis by the museum's education staff. A library, with full time staff, contains an extensive collection of books, records, mechanical engineering drawings, negatives and photographs and may be consulted by prior arrangement. There is also a museum shop which is much too small to satisfy the demands placed upon it.

The National Railway Museum is undoubtedly highly successful and popular – 1 million people visited it in its first ten months – and although it is too early to assess its long term user potential there can be little doubt that it will settle down to become one of the major museum attractions in the country. As an outstation of the Science Museum in London, under the charge of a Keeper and a very small staff, it has the advantages of links with a large parent institution without the disadvantages of total dominance by it. Of particular value has been the retention of the 'special relationship' with British Railways which must surely provide a sound foundation for future growth of the collections. Few people would now argue with the location of the museum in York and at a capital cost of about £1 million, excluding the site and old depot buildings which BR provided, it represents quite outstanding value for money. Comparison with other railway museums is difficult. Perhaps the nearest equivalent is the Baltimore railway museum originally developed by the Baltimore & Ohio Railroad and also housed in a roundhouse. Although the Baltimore building is greatly superior visually the quality of the display and more particularly the interpretation is infinitely higher in York. York's greatest asset is obviously its collection, of outstanding quality and importance, but its success to a great extent results from a level of presentation aimed quite consciously at the non–enthusiast. Here the influence of the Science Museum is clearly apparent and this is what sets York apart from so many railway museums all over the world which appear to have been designed by railwaymen for railwaymen.

References

1. *The Preservation of Relics and Records*: Report to the British Transport Commission (1951), para 6.
2. Ibid., para 8.

15 Museums, visitors - and what they expect

Handel Kardas

One of the hardest parts of running a museum these days is the human problem of trying to square the circle; how do you resolve the conundrum of reconciling the needs of the collection and your undisputed cultural and preservation role with the demands of visitors to enjoy their visit? This must come before even the other big conundrum of keeping expenditure within budget when there is a need to spend money on the existing collection and on worthy relics running out of time elsewhere and needing to be brought in.

A museum could, of course, decide to ignore the bulk of its visitors, concerning itself only with the cognoscenti and making the building up of its collection the paramount concern. But could it survive with this policy? Indeed, would it deserve to survive? For in the last analysis, a museum is there to present its collection to as large a part of the population as possible. In the context of the National Railway Museum, this could be taken to mean that the first–time visitor, who cares little for railways or their heritage as he steps through the entrance, is more important than the dedicated railway enthusiast who comes three times a year to spend a half–hour or so walking round his favourite locomotive (and plays hell if it has been taken off display for whatever reason).

Plate 15.1
The old York Railway Museum had a rather unprepossessing entrance and inside the exhibits were crammed into the space rather than laid out for display – but it gave such primeval artefacts as these a safe home for many years.

It is all, of course, a question of the rôle of the museum and it is possible to find a way through an apparent minefield if one remembers that the integrity of the collection is what matters. How it is presented and interpreted and the ancillaries developed around it are of lesser importance. For they can be changed to meet changing tastes and as long as nothing is done to an artefact that cannot readily be undone, there should be few rules in the pursuit of meeting changing tastes. Even – dare I say it – painting a face on *Mallard* should not be ruled forever out of order. It would, after all, do no structural damage to the loco, only aesthetic, and in restoring it to steamable condition a few years ago, far more original material was discarded and replaced than would be the case in a quick paint job. Not, I add, that I would want to see it – but one day the requirements of the National Railway Museum might justify even this.

Museums as places that attract substantial numbers of visitors have their roots in the Victorian age, when of course the great collections at South Kensington were established. The classic museum and the popular conception of museums that lasted until about a decade ago stem from that age, as places where relics were collected and put on display but generally kept out of reach of those who came to see them. They were places to walk round and look, and frequently the architecture encouraged and emphasized this role. They were places of cathedral proportions, where you were encouraged to walk round in a state of hush. Loud voices were firmly discouraged, running children would be admonished and shown the door if the running did not stop, exhibits did not do anything, the whole atmosphere was one of solemn learning. They served their purpose well and at the time they were revolutionary. In an age of limited opportunity for entertainment in leisure time and a more sober society when authority was generally accepted without question, museums were a great step forward. They brought an understanding of the past and its relevance to the present within the reach of most of the population. However, as society changed in the 20th century the bigger museums were on the whole ossified, becoming almost like their collections, a time warp within a time warp. As so often happens, the impetus for change came from outside and it was the massive growth of the leisure industry, giving people so many new ways of doing something active in their spare time, that eventually led museums to reconsider their approach.

The conservation of railway relics dates back to these early days of museums, though it was a very half–hearted affair for many years. South Kensington rescued some of the primeval machines, even saving the original, much–altered *Rocket*, and they still sit there in the Science Museum, smothered in what looks like black tar applied to preserve them without any attempt to put them into the condition of working machines. One suspects they would have gone under glass domes if the technology of the day had been up to it.

Various railway companies saved a few relics, mainly locomotives that were squirrelled away in quiet corners of workshops. A good demonstration of the attitude of the time was the fate of the broad gauge *Lord of the Isles* and *North Star*, scrapped at Swindon in the early Churchward era, not just because they were 'taking up much needed space' but because the GWR's attempt to find a new home for them failed. The Science Museum, among others, was simply not interested.

Otherwise, railway items in museums tended to be the silver spade used to cut the first sod of the local branch line, the wreath from Queen Victoria's funeral train and other such human–interest ephemera. The museums were reflecting the mood of their time, for railways were still not only commonplace but the current high technology. They were ubiquitous, used by and essential to everyone, and people did not expect to find their hardware on display in museum conditions.

In the context of respect for heritage the North Eastern Railway, with its successor the LNER, was a shining example, conscious of its size, importance and role as the cradle of railways. It not only kept more relics but took seriously the idea of a public display, which led to the formation of a railway museum in York in 1927. This solemn display, serried ranks of locomotives and a few odds and ends, was innovative in its way but very much a thing of its time. Relics were on display for the public to walk round and look. By all accounts, visitor figures were modest for many years. And the collection was, by current standards, unbalanced – lots of locomotives and precious little else. Probably most visitors until the early 1960s were enthusiasts, for railways were still very much a part of daily life. And in all honesty, the railway system had changed remarkably little from its Victorian zenith – and so many relics were in daily service that a museum containing more of them was not calculated to appeal to the mass of the population.

The mixed beginnings of massive decline and modernization of the railways brought about a sea–change in the public attitude, fired by the post–war growth in the number of railway enthusiasts. Many children went through a train–spotting phase and while they did not become enthusiasts in the accepted sense, many have retained a sympathetic, nostalgic interest ever since.

It was this sea–change that led to the building up of the National Railway Collection, primarily by the accumulation of recognised Historic Relics in the John Scholes era. We have a lot to thank this man for. He not only collected, he pushed the idea that such a collection should be available to the public. Thus was born Clapham Transport Museum and it must be said that it was an unduly conventional place, though this was hardly Scholes' fault. With a large collection of railway items and the severe limitations of a medium–size former tram depot to

Plate 15.3
The British Transport Museum at Clapham was a gloriously cluttered place. Somehow the feeling of it all being squeezed in gave it some appeal and the museum had a great atmosphere – but it was desperately too small for what it was expected to do.

display them in, it really was a question of squeezing things in as well as possible. No possibility of interpretation, of ready access to relics, of a hands–on approach were possible; and of course, a lot of items had to stay in store elsewhere. The public, however, reacted well. This museum was popular, especially with the young. It was certainly somewhere to take the children and it sticks in the mind as somewhere that bustled with life. Light and airy, with lots of visitors milling around, it was different from London's other museums. But people began to want more and the novelty of Clapham began to pall. The museum seemed quieter in its latter years than its first decade or so.

The planning for the permanent home for the National Collection took years before the National Railway Museum was finally agreed on, constructed and opened in York. Those of us who were taking an interest in the argument during those years will remember the passionate pleas in favour of various locations, the long drawn out debate and the demands of some that Clapham should at all costs be kept. The arguments, however, tended to come from the enthusiasts (many senior museum staff have learned to live with their outraged squawks when some 'vital' item is taken off display to let another in) and took little account of the fact that most visitors would be either politely interested or even arriving in a state of near ignorance, out of curiosity. Luckily, decisions were made by people with a wider view.

Plate 15.4
When this photograph inside York MPD was taken in the early 1960s, the photographer could hardly have guessed that the building was destined to become the heart of the National Railway Museum. At least it gave an air of authenticity!

So, how does the National Railway Museum stand in visitors' eyes now? The admission figures must tell part of the story and the fact that these have held up quite well despite the introduction of charges and then the trauma of having to undertake a massive rebuild, show that the museum's leaders have got things right to a reasonable degree at least. For the most potent publicity is by word of mouth and comments by satisfied – or dissatisfied – visitors to friends and neighbours can do far more than any advertising campaign ever can. Foremost in this bush telegraph system are the young visitors. Every museum curator should tremble at the sight of a 10–year old walking out muttering 'boring!', for he will probably put off another 50 potential visitors within 24 hours.

Remembering always that to be successful a museum needs to be popular and that to be popular it needs to be a tourist attraction, what must a museum such as the National Railway Museum do to meet the needs of its visitors and send them away feeling that it was time and money well spent?

The starting point must be the basics and these are the same for any tourist site. Access and comfort really must come high on the list. People want to be able to park easily and then start their the visit in a straightforward way; a short stroll, a dedicated bus or the like. Equally, good access by public transport is essential. Without this, the museum's chances of competing in the marketplace are much reduced. Many visitors will choose the soft option and go somewhere else, others arrive already disgruntled and in a mood to find faults. Once inside, good, varied refreshment facilities, clean, modern toilets, well–placed resting points and a variety of things to do with, ideally, nothing taking more than 15 minutes, are the essentials. These apply to any tourist attraction, be it a museum, a theme park, a fun fair or a stately home. Or, of course a preserved railway and it is in this area that the National Railway Museum has scored above many of these in the public eye. It is also much cleaner.

Where the National Railway Museum has been at a disadvantage against preserved lines is in the hands–on side of things. Railways are essentially semi–living things. Sound, smell and movement are part of their appeal. Except on special occasions, you cannot actually experience a ride on a moving train at the National Railway Museum and then not for very far. It has yet to prove possible for an engine to be in steam, or a diesel operating, every day, for instance.

Plate 15. 5
Some 20 years on from the previous photograph, the former running shed had changed dramatically. As unlikely a collection of locomotives as ever came together in York stand round the large turntable. The whole place has been thoroughly cleaned, losing, for the purist, its atmosphere, but the roof and layout are recognisable.

Against that, the unfortunate Derwent Valley experiment must be mentioned. In the early 1980s the then fast–fading, unnationalized, Derwent Valley Light Railway attempted to postpone oblivion by teaming up with the National Railway Museum to offer a combined package. Museum visitors could go on for a ride in a real steam train on the DVR. Joint marketing and bus connections offered great hopes but the scheme was a disappointment for the National Railway Museum and a fatal flop for the DVR. Why so?

One reason was certainly that at the time the National Railway Museum was free–admission. Having spent some time looking at trains for nothing, many people balked at more trains, for which they had to pay. Another reason, related to it, is that many visitors, having been to the National Railway Museum, had 'done trains'. They had had enough of this particular activity and wanted to go on and do something else. With so many other attractions to compete against, the DVR had little real chance.

This leads to another important point that the National Railway Museum has to consider; how long do people want to spend in the museum? There is a fine balance between feeling that it is all too big to take in and feeling you have got value for your money. Visitors must be able to get round the museum in a reasonable time – probably between an hour and a half and three hours. In simple terms, visitors will be prepared to give the National Railway Museum a half–day. Pricing can reflect this but only to an extent.

It is an interesting point that visitor numbers to the National Railway Museum fell when admission charges were introduced but the comment was made to me afterwards that they were tending to stay longer. Part of the value for money thing perhaps? And did the numbers fall because many visitors who had felt like popping in for an hour or so several times during their stay now came only once, paid and made sure they got full value out of it by spending a full morning there?

Visitors also expect something to do and reasonable access to exhibits these days. Here we have the great effect of other tourist attractions and the big–business input in a more leisured age making their effect. People who have been to theme parks or sampled the 'fast past' Jorvik and its like, no longer like traditional museums. Is it mere coincidence that the most popular exhibit in the old main hall was said to be the sectioned Bulleid Pacific locomotive? Here visitors could start to understand what a steam engine is all about. Perhaps the next innovation should be a sectioned Class 47 diesel, a move which would doubtless cause as much of a fuss as sectioning the Bulleid locomotive did!

Here we need to look very hard at the changes which have taken place at the National Railway Museum in the last few years, since the great rebuilding started. The redesign of the main hall so that it becomes a properly–controllable exhibition building designed for optimum conservation of its contents, caused one of the regular furores from enthusiasts that have marked the National Collection's existence. A refusal to see the building as a housing for the collection, insisting rather that it was a relic in its own right, had a factual basis but did not take into account the relative values of the National Collection and a rather degenerate example of roundhouse design and construction. Its status as a two–table roundhouse, the last one left, was not enough to endear it to the typical visitor and, equally important, it could not be made into a selling point. There are preserved railways which have discovered that by charging a premium fare you can get visitors to relish travelling in your oldest, wooden–seated, Victorian coaches and realise that they have done something special. But the old main hall did not have the sort of atmosphere to make this possible. Too clearly it looked what it was; a 1950s concrete roofed building from one of the worst eras in British architecture.

The Peter Allen building, by contrast, has proved to be 'sellable' to visitors. For long an El Dorado to which only the privileged guests were invited (and they then

Plate 15.6
The entrance of the Great Railway Show set the right atmosphere from the moment a visitor arrived at the entrance

Plate 15.7
The Peter Allen Building gave the Great Railway Show a spendidly appropriate atmosphere which caught the imaginations of visitors. Conceived as an emergency stop gap measure, it has been such a success that a similar style of display will be put on here as a permanent feature after Great Hall reopens

told the tale to enthusiast friends, watching them go green with envy!), it looks like the popular conception of a vintage railway building. Its choice as the home for the temporary exhibition was obvious and the layout was inspired. Although a former goods shed, not a passenger station, it nonetheless lent itself well to a representation of a bustling terminus.

Having, so to speak, made a virtue out of a necessity, the National Railway Museum went the whole hog with something of a 'theme park' approach. The impressions formed by enthusiasts have been mixed (and in many cases preconceived) but the effect on typical visitors has been impressive. They enjoy it. Here, laid out, is a clear impression of what railways are all about. Footplates are visible, some are accessible, you can see into the coaches and go into some of them, there are wagons, station furniture, displays of small relics, a whole world of railway history under one roof. Outside, the large 'tent' has given a more formal display of locomotives but to me the finest part of all was Magician's Road – the "classroom" for the Museum's education service. I visited this area when a visiting school party was in full cry and I cannot praise it too highly. With models to play with and learn in the process how signalling works, a locomotive to stand on, a small steam plant to demonstrate how it works, a bridge building kit and plenty more, the National Railway Museum has a really valuable section here, that can teach children more about railways than any number of more conventional museums.

This begs the question – fine, but is it what visitors *expect*? The answer is that most of the National Railway Museum's visitors arriving for the first time do not know *what* to expect. They know it is something about trains, which means, as it is a museum, old trains. Which, so far, still means steam. They expect to find it interesting and they expect it to be a comfortable and convenient place to spend a few hours. In the last couple of years, thanks to the Great Railway Show (and the word 'Great' was a brilliant piece of marketing) they expect something on a par with the other big cultural attractions in and around York. They do not expect a dry, dusty museum and they are not let down in this. Otherwise, they arrive as largely green, unworked material and it is up to the museum to work this to its advantage and make the most of what it can offer.

Plate 15.8
The new roof and revised track layout has changed Great Hall almost beyond recognition. How visitors will react remains to be seen but the sense of spaciousness will be envied by many museums with collections of large relics

For the future, it has to be said that the National Railway Museum has made a rod for its own back. Having staged the Great Railway Show, there can be no turning back, even to the 1980s, which were a great advance on what had gone before. Something like the Show, an interpretative display on the grand scale, must be kept or visitors who have seen, or heard of it, will go away disappointed. Which will be fatal. Luckily this has always been the plan. The rebuild of the main hall has been an opportunity for an expansive drive at the National Railway Museum and unbiased observers will agree that the opportunity has been seized with both hands.

Finally, we need to consider what the enthusiasts expect of the National Railway Museum. The trouble here is that there are almost as many variations in this as there are enthusiasts. But to the serious enthusiast, York has two key functions and it has performed them well. Firstly it is an active collector of railway heritage and makes it as accessible as possible. Secondly it has a massive and growing archive of photographs, drawings and published material and is a place where serious research and study can be carried out at no charge in the Museum's Library Reading Room, though space and staff constraints at the Museum mean that access to the archive cannot be totally open. In this, of course, the Museum is at one with others – the archive is available to serious researchers.

Enthusiasts do have an important role to play in encouraging, in various ways, the National Railway Museum to expand its activities. They know what could be displayed in a way which the average visitor does not. Thus, a good display of signalling equipment is something which many enthusiasts have asked for – the typical visitor does not realise that he is missing out in this. Enthusiasts have encouraged and helped the National Railway Museum in its policy of lending out items, from the smallest to the largest. Again, the typical visitor will not be aware that as many locomotives as are on display are loaned out to other centres and to railways. There are, of course, the other enthusiasts, who cry out for a museum housing the entire National Collection on the mausoleum principle, but the National Railway Museum has always had and used the ability to discern between different types of enthusiast, to work with the visionaries and placate or override the harpers. This is one of its strengths.

Looking ahead, it would be foolish to try to guess at how public tastes will change. The National Railway Museum must be prepared to change with them or be marginalised. And this would be to fail in its duty. More than any preserved railway, the National Railway Museum has a central role, which is to educate, gently, through interest and entertainment as appropriate, as many people as possible into the heritage of our railways. It is doing so with increasing skill. If in the future it can continue to adapt its style to suit public tastes while guarding its primary function of protecting the integrity of its collection and also keeping alive the possibility for serious study into all aspects of railway history, it will be serving the country well. And that means that in the future, it may well be one of the breeding grounds for new generations of active preservationists. The National Railway Museum has the potential to create enthusiasts. And all existing enthusiasts, particularly those who value the past, owe it a debt of gratitude and should aim to encourage it in its work.

16 "All Change" - new buildings and displays at the National Railway Museum, 1988-1992

Rob Shorland–Ball

"All Change" at a railway station heralds the end of a journey. For the National Railway Museum "all change" has meant the start of a new journey – a journey which, by 1992, has replaced all the Museum's original displays, doubled the public display space and provided for visitors a far more comprehensive evocation of the story of railways past, present and future. A journey moreover which even in 1992 will not be complete for the Museum has plans and proposals to sustain and enhance its role as an international leader among railway museums into the 21st century.

It is convenient for the present purpose to consider the four years from 1988 to 1992, since during that time the most profound changes in the Museum's history have taken place. The National Railway Museum opened in York in 1975 and by 1988 had expanded to occupy an area of some 15 acres bisected by a busy road – Leeman Road. Plate 16.1 shows the two principal groups of buildings. The original public display area in 1975 – the Main Hall – and the adjoining workshops and stores together with the museum offices, lecture theatre and reference library lie to the south east of Leeman Road. Across the road is the former York Goods Station, now the Peter Allen Building, and used as a museum store since 1976 but purchased with the long–term aim of being opened to the

public. It must be remembered that "store" in the National Railway Museum context means not only small–object storage but rail–connected buildings capable of holding items up to 70 ft long and weighing over 100 tons. Beyond the Museum's principal buildings are several acres of sidings and connections to British Rail's operating network.

Curatorial staff had been working for some time on display proposals for the Peter Allen building. In 1987 a consultant architect, Dr Roger Wools, and Robin Wade, the internationally known museum and exhibition designer, collaborated on a report which has provided a blue–print underpinning the changes and developments that have evolved over the past four years. In 1988, Dr Cossons, Director of the National Museum of Science and Industry of which the National Railway Museum is a part, made a formal announcement of long–term development plans at York based on the proposals in the Wade/Wools Report. Included were:

> a **pedestrian subway** under Leeman Road linking the two areas of the Museum described above;

> a new **Main Entrance** building on the Peter Allen side of Leeman Road incorporating visitor services including retailing. The subway under Leeman Road would lead from this building to:

> an **Introductory Gallery** adjacent to the existing Main Hall and covering the site of the adjoining open area. The subway from the Entrance Building would emerge in the basement of the Introductory Gallery. The Gallery would provide an interpretative introduction to railways – and particularly to the social and economic impact of the railway revolution – and to the two principal display areas which would be:

> the renamed **Great Hall** (formerly the Main Hall), with displays rearranged to encompass the technology of the railways but also reflecting the social and economic history.

> the renamed **South Hall** (the offices at the front of the building would retain the Peter Allen name) where the existing layout of parallel railway tracks separated by platforms offered the opportunity to illustrate the process of travelling by train for passengers and for goods.

The reference library and archive and the public reading and reference room would be enhanced and would both underpin and reinforce the scholarly basis on which the magnificent objects forming the National Railway Collection would be interpreted and presented to the public.

Dr Cossons' announcement of these exciting and far–reaching proposals was made on 3 July 1988 during the celebrations of the 50th anniversary of the locomotive *Mallard's* world speed record for steam traction of 126 mph. It was known, however, that the Museum's discussions with the Office of Arts & Libraries and the Treasury about funding for the development were likely to be protracted and the development plans would not move forward with such startling speed. Although curatorial planning was well in hand a realistic start date seemed a little remote.

The catalyst which brought about the changes described in this paper was the Main Hall roof. It had been known for some years that the concrete beams in the roof were failing and the development plans included financial provision for a replacement. Once it was established by the structural engineers that work on the roof must start by April 1990 all forward planning took on a new and particular urgency.

It is important to appreciate the scale of the roof works. The Main Hall covers an area of 2 acres and the existing 1950s roof consisted of two central arched pitches and 6 smaller pitches forming side roofs on horizontal concrete beams and supported by a forest of columns. No less than 14 valley gutters drained the roof and several of them leaked into the display area. The roof had minimal insulation and more than 50% was glazed producing very high UV levels, solar gain in summer and heat loss in the winter. The concrete beams which formed the structure were cast from a high–chloride content cement which was valued in the 1950s for its quick–drying properties. It is now known that especially in the presence of moisture the chlorides accelerate rusting of the reinforcing rods in the beams causing eventual structural failure.

The Architectural Team for the roof works was entirely York based:

Architect	Dr Roger Wools, Alex Gordon Partnership (York)
Engineer:	Mark Stevenson, Gifford & Partners (York)
Quantity Surveyor:	Ian Busby, Turner and Holman (York)

Plate 16.2
The new roof of the Great Hall during construction in 1991 showing the massive steel ridge beam.

The Architect's brief to re–roof soon evolved into an attempt to solve the many problems of the existing roof. The solution – one pitch covering the whole Hall and supported by a massive steel ridge beam carried on two end buttresses and a central pillar – is both elegant and visually dramatic (Plate 16.2). Even more important it provides a clear floor area for displays and greatly improves sight lines across the Hall from first floor level.

Replacing the roof, however, was only one part of the equation. The Main Hall was the principal public display area of the Museum and it was soon apparent that major repairs, priceless objects and visitors could not co–exist. There were, three options:

> i. To close the whole Museum for the period of the roof works;

> ii. To retain a partial public presence centred on the reference library and the art gallery which were not affected by the roof works;

> iii. To take advantage of the opportunities offered by the roof works and test a number of the development project proposals by bringing forward the opening of a new exhibition in the South Hall during the roof rebuilding.

After examining all the options carefully, the third one was chosen. The decision was made to move the public activities of the Museum (with the exception of the Library which remained open) over the road into the South Hall: thus was born The Great Railway Show (Plate 16.3). Fortunately a great deal of curatorial planning had already gone towards the development proposals for the Peter Allen Building and a York curatorial team was in existence to take the plans forward. Robin Wade worked with the York team as the lead designer and his experience added an invaluable extra dimension.

In the sense that a catalyst promotes a reaction the roof works have indeed been seminal: the necessity to repair the roof provided the opportunity to create The Great Railway Show, underlined the need to provide a dedicated crossing of Leeman Road for visitors (the subway) and secured some emergency funding from the Office of Arts and Libraries, the Government body which funds the National Museums.

The planning authority – York City Council – have been very supportive of all the National Railway Museum's development proposals but the planners made clear that visitors must have a safe means of crossing Leeman Road and the subway was an ideal solution.

Another vital element to be resolved was the storage of items not displayed in the Great Railway Show but displaced from the Main Hall which had to be completely emptied. The cost of commercial storage for large items like railway locomotives was considerable and thus the notion of The National Railway Museum on Tour at an appropriate location was conceived. The location proved to be Swindon, in association with Tarmac Properties Ltd who are developing the site of the former Swindon Railway Workshops. It is a measure of the richness of the National Railway Collection and of the amount of material in store and not on display that two large exhibitions could be created, at York and Swindon. In 1990 more of the Collection was on public display than has ever previously been the case.

The various elements of change at York made a formidable project and at a formidable cost. The Great Railway Show, the National Railway Museum on Tour, the Leeman Road subway and the Main Hall roof repairs were originally costed at £5.7 million. The Office of Arts & Libraries provided £2.0 million but the remainder had to come from the National Museum of Science & Industry's revenue budget and finding it proved a daunting task. The Trustees of the Museum finally approved a total budget of £5.0 million (requiring an immediate saving of £700,000 on the York proposals) but still leaving a total of £3.0 million to be found 'in house'. The consequence over the whole Museum was to halt virtually all project and development work save for that at York which was an inevitable disappointment for colleagues who saw their own plans postponed or cancelled. At the National Railway Museum, however, the staff were very conscious of the privilege and the responsibility that attached to undertaking probably the most comprehensive re–organisation ever undertaken by a major national museum without a period of total closure to the public.

The urgency of the need to repair the roof imposed an exacting discipline on the Museum's Project Team. Planning permission for the subway under Leeman Road and the changed use of the South Hall from storage to display was granted in June 1989. Subway construction started in September of the same year and had to be completed by February 1990. On the last day of February the Main Hall closed to the public as usual at 1800 hrs and at 1000 hrs the following morning the Great Railway Show opened to visitors in the South Hall. A month was available to completely strip out the Main Hall and to complete the complicated logistics of moving 40 locomotives and items of rolling stock by rail or road to Swindon. On 1 April the Main Hall was handed over to the contractors: as demolition began, the total collapse of a 5–ton concrete roof beam emphasised the urgency of the timetable set by the results of the structural engineer's earlier inspection. On 10 April 1990 The National Railway Museum on Tour opened in Swindon.

The Great Railway Show represented a complete change in display philosophy for the Museum. The South Hall is a very atmospheric building and, in its resemblance to a railway terminus, (though with higher platforms than a passenger station) provides a ready sense of identification for visitors who are, for the most part, not knowledgeable railway enthusiasts. Visitors see a Midland Railway dining car express, or a London & South Western Railway suburban train, or the magnificent London & North Western Railway Royal Train in a station setting which is familiar and which can stimulate the imagination and, for some, the memory. The setting provides a more obvious opportunity than previously to tell the human story of the railways. For the first time a short goods train is displayed and some tenth of the entire space is devoted to freight which is particularly appropriate in a former Goods Station building (Plate 16.4). The modern railway is not forgotten either and generous sponsorship from Balfour Beatty Power Construction and Hornby Hobbies has provided, respectively, a section of 25Kv overhead catenary and a model railway layout on which only modern diesel and electric trains operate.

Plate 16. 4
The freight section of the Great Railway Show.

Visitor clinics before the exhibition opened and subsequent visitor surveys have shown clearly that the format of the exhibition is popular. Access to vehicles, a station platform restaurant, sound effects, staff in period costume, a Royal Train and operating locomotives in the South Yard behind the hall are all in accord with visitor expectations and must all have helped the exhibition to gain the 1991 National Heritage Museum of the Year Award.

Plate 16.5
"Magician's Road", the
Museum education
department's interactive
exhibition.

The Project Team, and Robin Wade as the lead designer, gave a great deal of thought to interpreting the displays. A very tight budget ultimately limited ambition but within that constraint a Railway Chronology, panel and lectern texts and photographs, slides, video and sound effects have all been used – but deliberately not obtrusively. It was felt that labels on carriages and locomotives would destroy the illusion of a railway station. There are, however, extensive descriptive and historical notes about the objects on lecterns and panels set back on the platforms.

Information in the exhibition has been complemented by publications including an extensive Teachers' Handbook which provides a general introduction to railways and a number of worksheets. Education work at the Museum is another area where "all change" has meant a new beginning. From 1975 until 1990 the Education Service operated a very competent but increasingly rather dated service centred round a Lecture Theatre (complete with an AV screen and a demonstration bench) and Gallery Tours in the Main Hall. Following some very constructive debate, a new educational interactive area was set up in a small goods shed adjoining the South Hall and called Magician's Road (The railway ".... proved a Magician's Road. The locomotive gave a new celerity to time. It virtually reduced England to a sixth of its size ..." Samuel Smiles writing in 1903). The area contains a number of practical demonstrations of railway engineering – signalling, bridge–building, streamlining, a locomotive cab – for use by booked school parties. It has proved very popular and as money allows, is being improved and developed (Plate 16.5).

The imperative of the roof repairs did not prevent forward planning for the full development first outlined in 1988. Indeed, there was some hope that the Introductory Gallery and new Main Entrance could follow on – perhaps as a linked project with the same contractor – from the roof works. The problem of finance was, however, exacerbated by the drain on the overall Museum revenue budget caused by the need to fund the balance of the roof works beyond the grant aid offered by the Office of Arts & Libraries. It was agreed that any further development at York must not be at the expense of work elsewhere within the whole National Museum of Science & Industry and particularly at the Science Museum itself. The proposed solution, to borrow the money and repay capital and interest from the incremental income generated by additional visitors, is without precedent for a National Museum and is therefore proving especially difficult to negotiate.

Meanwhile the contractors were busy with the huge task of re–roofing the Main Hall, and the Project Team – whose task included creating the new displays in the Hall – were debating a number of options including two which raised great anger in some parts of the railway enthusiast press.

Plate 16.6
Aerial view (looking west) showing the Great Hall roof in 1957/8 at the start of work by BR on the replacement concrete roof which was, in turn, replaced by the present steel structure. The adjoining diesel depot roof is almost complete. The 1957/8 BR roof is shown complete in Plate 16.1 before demolition and rebuilding began.

The original building which became the National Railway Museum in 1975 was a 19th century steam locomotive shed which ultimately, in the two offset but adjoining rectangular buildings seen clearly in Plate 16.6, contained four turntables. Like all such buildings it grew and changed organically with use. On 29 April 1942 the shed received a direct hit from a bomb which did considerable damage to the structure. Patching carried the building through until a major rebuilding by British Railways in 1957/8. The part of the shed nearest the main line was demolished, the two turntables were removed and the whole rebuilt as a straight–road shed and repair shop for diesel locomotives. It is now the Museum's workshop and stores.

What became the Museum's Main Hall retained its two turntables but was otherwise almost completely rebuilt including the multi–pitch concrete roof that failed in 1990. In preparation for Museum use further structural changes were made in 1973/4 including the insertion of a full length mezzanine gallery. The interior was thoroughly cleaned and painted and, save for the cognoscenti, the ambience of a steam locomotive shed was lost. Even the smoke hoods which were replaced over some of the turntable roads were fibreglass replicas and were more confusing for not actually penetrating the roof cladding. Once opened to the public, a number of visitors who were quite unaware of the origins of the building commented on the ingenuity of the Museum's architects in installing turntables to display the locomotives and rolling stock.

It was apparent to the Project Team that the roof works offered the only chance in the foreseeable future to make any physical changes to the appearance and layout of the Hall. The decision to replace the 1950s concrete multi–pitch roof with a new single pitch steel one was not too difficult. The integrity of the original building was damaged by the wartime bombing, greatly compromised by the BR rebuild in the 1950s and virtually expunged by the Museum building works in the 1970s. The opportunity to create a railway–like structure – with a span at eaves level similar to that of the great arch of St Pancras – that was relatively maintenance free, insulated and left an uncluttered floor area was irresistible.

The decision to change the track geometry by removing the smaller of the two turntables was much more difficult. There was never any doubt that the most dramatic, effective and appropriate way to display a large collection of steam locomotives was round a turntable. The display of rolling stock and, particularly, long carriages, round the second turntable was arguably less successful. Carriages were not usually stored in that way on the working railway; they presented a rather unattractive array of carriage ends to the viewer on the turntable; the cone–shaped spaces in between the radial tracks were awkward to use for small objects; and the short track lengths throughout the Hall meant that trains – or even 2–car multiple units – were almost impossible to accommodate.

Removing one turntable could overcome these problems and provide longer, straighter tracks for short trains, multiple units or temporary exhibitions of visiting locomotives and rolling stock. It would provide visual relief in the layout of the Hall and lead the visitor from the new entrance at the south end of the Hall through the tracks to the piece–de–resistance of the locomotive display. Against this was the uniqueness of the two–turntable engine shed layout but on the other hand there had to be an assessment of the relative importance of the steam locomotive and its engine shed to the overall railway story the Museum seeks to tell.

So the discussion waxed and waned and, lest it be thought that the Museum staff act alone in such matters, the decision to remove the turntable was considered by Dr Cossons, by the National Railway Museum Advisory Committee and, by report, by the Board of Trustees. The case for any significant change can always be argued in more than one way. History, and the visitor reaction to the redisplayed Hall will provide a measure of judgement on the turntable decision. Suffice it to say that the decision was reached after careful debate and reflection and a mature consideration of the overall purpose and needs of the Museum.

Before concluding with a brief description of the re–roofed Great Hall displays it is necessary to backtrack a little. The success of the South Hall displays that were evolved for the Great Railway Show, their complementary nature in relation to the proposals for the Great Hall, and the need to provide more public display space for the National Railway Collection all argued strongly for the retention of the South Hall as a public display area when the Great Hall was re–opened. Indeed, that was precisely what was envisaged in the overall development proposals but, with the proviso that the new Main Entrance/Introductory Gallery complex of buildings would need substantial funding. It became apparent, therefore, that to close the South Hall in order to re–open the Great Hall was a retrograde step and so was born the First Step project. The "First Step" is towards a fully consolidated museum which, as other steps can be funded, will include the Introductory Gallery, workshop viewing facilities, East Coast Main Line viewing gallery and much more. For the moment First Step means a new Main Entrance (Plate 16.7) and a substantial move towards an entirely redisplayed and interpreted Great Hall. The work was completed for a Royal opening of the new, enlarged National Railway Museum by HRH the Duke of Kent on Thursday 16 April 1992.

Plate 16.7
The new Main Entrance which links the two Halls together through the subway under Leeman Road.

The South Hall displays have not changed greatly from those which constituted the Great Railway Show. The underlying theme is still travel by train for goods and people. The two recently acquired 19th century oil paintings by George Earl, Going North (at King's Cross) and Coming South (at Perth) are displayed at York for the first time as part of an introduction to the exhibition. There are more Royal carriages, some minor changes elsewhere and a gradual enhancing of Magician's Road.

In the Great Hall the complementary theme is the "materiel" of railways under the generic title of the technology of the railways. It covers the great variety of objects which make up the National Railway Collection and range from a ticket to a locomotive by way of uniforms, medals, silver, china, printed ephemera, drawings (both technical and otherwise), prints, posters, architectural ironwork, permanent way, signalling and much else besides.

Most visitors, using the new Main Entrance and the subway, will enter Great Hall at the south end. The immediate visual impression is of great height. Advantage has been taken of the height to erect several large railway structures which help to create a sense of scale both for the railway vehicles and for the Hall itself. Most dramatic is a twenty–four foot diameter concrete ring from the Channel Tunnel, complete with track, services and overhead catenary. The ring, which marks the largest construction project in Europe this century, also reflects the Museum's intention to display contemporary as well as historic objects (Plate 16.8). Immediately beyond the Tunnel and continuing the theme of today's railways is a special exhibition sponsored by British Rail: "A Railway for Today and Tomorrow". It is designed to be regularly changed and updated.

Plate 16.8
The Channel Tunnel exhibit in the Great Hall.

Elsewhere in the south part of the Hall an eight doll signal gantry from Northolt Junction and the cast iron North Eastern Railway footbridge from Percy Main station near Newcastle both help to give a sense of scale to railway artefacts. The vehicles themselves appear enormous to the visitor at floor level but the perception changes when they are seen under the gantry or the footbridge. It changes again when the visitor climbs the footbridge to see across the Hall from an appropriate railway vantage point (Plate 16.9).

Plate 16.9
A North Eastern Railway cast iron footbridge of 1891 restored and erected in the Great Hall by the Museum workshops.

Visitors are free to roam at will for there is no pre-ordained route but gently curving tracks at the south end of the Hall do inevitably lead the eye and feet towards the display of locomotives grouped chronologically round the turntable. They are enhanced by the sectioned locomotive *Ellerman Lines*, its wheels and motion turned by electricity, which caused much favourable comment in the "old" museum.

For visitors who like a sense of ordered progression the permanent way display serves as a time line linking the north and south ends of the Hall. A continuous welded rail on concrete, wood and steel sleepers and spanned by a section of overhead catenary adjoins the Channel Tunnel and British Rail displays. Successive sections of flat bottom, bull–head, fish–bellied and plate rail show how a little regarded but vital element of the railway has changed through time.

Signalling, too, is given more space in the new displays than was possible in the former Main Hall. A working demonstration of two audible warning systems for drivers, the Great Western Automatic Train Control and BR's Automatic Warning System, helps to explain why rail travel is inherently very safe.

Smaller or more delicate objects such as uniforms, original artwork and posters, silver, china, medals, tickets and models will be displayed on the mezzanine gallery which will re–open to visitors in the Autumn of 1992. An award from the Museum and Galleries Improvement Fund has allowed a restructuring of the long rows of showcases on the gallery and the creation of more flexible display spaces.

The Easter 1992 opening of the new Main Entrance, Great Hall and new displays in a public area twice the size of that in 1975 was a station on the Museum's journey of development and a convenient destination for this particular account. It is certainly not the terminus, however, for there are more changes and developments to come. It has been a great privilege to lead the Museum project team which has brought about the changes described in this paper. The Museum staff take great pride in the new National Railway Museum that they have helped to create and which gives the visitor a more complete picture of the magician's road which Samuel Smiles rightly perceived the railway to be.

Plate 16.10
An aerial view (looking north) of the new National Railway Museum opened by HRH the Duke of Kent on Thursday 16 April 1992. The new Great Hall roof provides an interesting contrast with Plates 16.1 and 16.6.

BIOGRAPHIES
OF
CONTRIBUTORS

Richard Durack: Curator of Archive and Pictorial Collections at the National Railway Museum since 1983. Formerly Assistant Archivist with Tyne and Wear Archives department. Co-author (with Beverley Cole) of *Happy as a Sandboy* (Railway Posters before 1923) and *Railway Posters 1923-1948*.

Philip Atkins: Librarian at the National Railway Museum since 1975. Author of a number of articles and books on locomotive development and history.

Christine J Heap: Curator of Information Services at the National Railway Museum since 1989. Formerly Archivist at the Science Museum, London 1985-1989 and Assistant Keeper (Archives) at the Museum of Science & Industry, Manchester 1977-1985.

Michael Rutherford: Curator of Engineering Drawings at the National Railway Museum since 1975. Following an electrical engineering apprenticeship, worked for a number of years on industrial instrumentation and control systems.

Michael Robbins: London Transport 1939-80 (managing director, railways 1971-78); author of *The North London Railway* (1937); *The Railway Age* (1962); *George & Robert Stephenson* (1966); (with T C Barker) *A History of London Transport I*, 1963, *II*, 1974. Member of the National Railway Museum Advisory Committee since 1978.

David Mosley: Education Officer at the National Railway Museum since 1979. Co-author of *Fifteen Inch Gauge Railways – their history, equipment and operation* (1986). Chairman of the Ravenglass & Eskdale Railway Preservation Society.

Arthur J Lowe: Research Chemist and Manager, ICI 1940-70. Life Member, Stephenson Locomotive Society. Council Member of the Friends of the National Railway Museum from inception and Editor of the FNRM *Newsletter* from 1979.

Dick Riley: Dick Riley's first railway photographs were taken with a Box Brownie in 1935. He has undertaken several photo research projects for the National Railway Museum. Now retired from banking, he has published a number of collections of his work.

Dieter Hopkin: Curator of Collections at the National Railway Museum since 1989. Post graduate research: "Railway Preservation: Museums & Enthusiasts", Leicester University 1987.

Helen Ashby: Assistant Curator of Collections at the National Railway Museum since 1983. Author of several articles and papers on aspects of the Museum's collections.

David Wright: Curator at the Science Museum, London 1974–1989. Currently Assistant Curator of Collections at the National Railway Museum.

Beverley Cole: Curator of the Pictorial Collection at the National Railway Museum and formerly a curator at the National Museum of Photography, Film and Television in Bradford.

Richard Gibbon: Curator of Engineering at the National Railway Museum since 1989. Formerly Assistant Keeper at Kelham Island Industrial Museum, Sheffield

Neil Cossons: Director of the National Museum of Science & Industry since 1986. Formerly Director of the Ironbridge Gorge Trust and of the National Maritime Museum.

Handel Kardas: Editor of Railway World and a lifelong railway enthusiast. Interested in railway history and heritage. An active preservationist for over twenty years.

Rob Shorland-Ball: Deputy Head of the National Railway Museum since 1987 and Project Manager for the Museum's £6.5M re–roofing and re–display. Formerly Director of the 70–acre Museum of East Anglian Life in Suffolk.

Allan Patmore: Emeritus Professor of Geography at the University of Hull, Vice Chairman of the Sports Council, member of the National Railway Museum Advisory Committee and Chairman of the Friends of the NRM.

LIST
OF
SUBSCRIBERS

Subscribers are listed by name and title. Degrees, decorations etc, have not been included.

Abbott, Mark Peter
Adams, J F
Adams, R H
Adams, Richard
Addyman, Peter and Shelly
Alderson, Catherine
Alexander, John
Alex Gordon Partnership
Allen, D A
Allen, Sir Peter
Amey, J J
Anderson, Dr. C K
Anspach, Dr. Denny S,
Appleyard, Ian S
Archer, Jack
Ashton, C H
Asselberghs, Marie–Anne
Association of Railway
  Preservation Societies
Atkinson, P J
Austin, Barry
Awdry, Christopher
Awdry, Rev W V
Ayers, Robert J
Ball, Edward
Banfield, A
Bannister, Keith
Barber, John
Barberis, Rex A
Barnard, Peter
Barraclough, D B G
Barrett, Ernest C,
Bearman, G W
Beckett, Thomas
Beechey, Peter J C
Bell, Martin L
Bell, Philip E
Bell, R L
Bellamy, Arthur H
Berry, John C
Biddle, Gordon
Blakeborough, David
Bootland, Philip
Bradbourne, Walter
Brading, Colin
Bradsell, Jeremy
Broadhead, D P
Broadley, Dennis N
Brown, Rupert D E
Bryan, Tim
Burton, M T
Burton, Nigel R
Busby, Ian G K
Butler, S W
Bysouth, J
California State
  Railroad Museum
Card, Roy A J
Carter, I A R
Causebrook, R J
Charlesworth, Leslie
Chesterman, Rev Canon Tony

Christie, E M, Director,
  Viking Hotel,York
Clabby, Mick
Clegg, Terence
Cliff, Rev F A,
Cole, Edward Harry
Combes, Martin
Conrad, Dr-Ing Dietrich
Cook, Charles W F
Cooke, N A
Cooling, C P
Copson, William Stuart
Corfield, A B
Cossons, Neil
Crane, Derek J
Crossley, Granville
Cully, J V R
Davies & Metcalfe plc
Dawson, John B
Day, J T
Dean, Michael C H
Denholm, Michael J
de Rothschild, Leopold
Deutsches Museum
Dewhurst, Roger Hutton
Dill–Russell, Scott William
Dingwall, W J
Dixey, S John
Dixon, J B
Dixon, John F
Dodd, Michael William
Doerr, Michel
Dow, Andrew
Downe, The Viscount
Draper, T J
Duckenfield, M J
Dunn, Terry J
Dyckhoff, N F W
Dyke, Steven G
Edgington, John
Edlington, R
Edmondson, Richard H
Ellerton, D E
Ellis, Elwyn
Ellis, Graham E
Esau, Mike
Evans, Jeremy
Fairburn, S
Ford, Colin
Foster, Eric L
Foster, G I
Fox, Gary W
Fox, Prof. Robert
Foxton, Greta
Frank, John F K
Fussey, Jack
Gray, Walter P, III
Great Western Enterprise Limited
Great Western Railway Museum
Green, Peter
Greenwood, William
Gretton, Richard F

Griffin–Smith, David
Grimthorpe, Lord
Hall, J Desmond
Hall, Stanley
Hall–Patch, Tony
Hamilton, Geoffrey
Hanenbergh, Hans
Harden, Peter L
Harding, B J
Harding, Michael
Harris, Nigel
Harvey, D W
Haslar, Wallace G
Heath, D L
Hector, Gordon
Hemley, John
Hepworth, Alan
Hervey–Bathurst, James
Heughan, G Walter K
Hill, Andrew
Hinchcliffe, George Durant
Hines, J M
Hirai, Masato
Hopton, Sydney T
Horner, Brian M K
Humm, Robert
Hunt, John Patrick
IMAX Corporation
International Association of
  Transport Museums
Isaacs, Leon Jonathan
Jackson, D T
Jackson, Dr. Norman Vincent
James, D H
Jarrold Publishing
Jefford, Philip
Johnson, Ian
Jones, K A
Jones, Richard Huxley
Jux, David (Butlins Ltd)
Kemp, Colin
Kerrin, Rev A E
Kershaw, Peter
Killick, A R
Knowles, Gordon
Kozlekedesi Muzeum Budapest
Lacey, Brian
Langridge, E A
Langstaff, Alan
Larke, John
Launder, G W
Linsley, Robin
Loasby, Brian J
Lowe, Arthur J
Lugg, Peter J
Lumb, Edna
Macdonald, Patrick
Malton, B A
Manchester Museum of
  Science & Industry
Manisty, Peter V,
Mann, Diana

Martin, R W
Martin, Stuart
Max, Michael G
McAlpine, The Hon Sir William Bt
McKenna & Co
Meadows, Gordon
Merrill, Eric
Mitchell, Peter
Mizushima, Toru
Montagu, of Beaulieu, Lord
Moore, John S
Morgan, David T
Murray, A
Musee Francais du Chemin
   de Fer, Mulhouse
Needler, R F
Nelson, Aidan
Newsome, J E
Nicholls, Robert V V
Nile, Roy
North Eastern Locomotive
   Preservation Group
Ovenstone, Peter R
Page, Walter
Palm, Jim (BBC Local Radio)
Parham, Martin N
Parker, Bill
Paterson, Frank
Patmore, J Allan
Pearson, D M
Pearson, Graham R
Peck, John
Pemberton, Robert T
Pettitt, Gordon
Phillipson, George
Pigott, Nick
Piper, Stephen
Platts, John
Pope, Gordon R
Porter, Keith
Porter, W A
Pracy, Dr. J P
Preston, H P
Prospervision
Ransom, P J G
Rayner, A G
Reader, Aubrey A
Rebernik, Peter
Reeves, Steven K
Revell, C A W
Rey, Fredy
Reynolds, W O
Rice, D J
Richards, G W
Richards, R StJ
Richardson, W
Richmond–Brown, Sir Charles
Riddick, Julian & Robert
Ridealgh, Michael
Riley, Peter
Rimmer, John
Rodgers, Peter J

Rose, M R
Rowntree, Richard S
Royston, W S
Ruddy, John R
Runeckles, A L
Russell, Prof. Colin
Russell, E S
Rutter, George M
Satow, M G
Saunders, Alan D
Saville, J Michael
Sawyer, Derek
Schippers, Rob
Scott, Alistair
Scott, Andrew J
Searle, Matthew
Sell, Robin
Semmens, Peter W B
Sewell, Ivor A
Shaw, Geoffrey W
Shepherd, Donald
Shorland–Ball, Rob
Sills, David
Simmons, Jack
Sinclair, Neil T
Smith, Bill
Smith, Cecil L
Smith, J B E
Smith, Leslie G
Soane, Leslie J
Spiers, Robert D
St John–Smith, Emma
Stansfield, Dr. E V
Steadman, A
Stephens, D A
Stonor, David
Straker, J M W
Swedish National Railway Museum
Tarrant, Bernard
Taylor, K D
Taylor, Richard Keevil
Thistleton, Cllr. F H
Thomas, David
Tillotson, David B
Tinker, Richard J A
Tomlinson, Harold P
Townley, Raymond
Travis, Peter
Tsujii, Jun
Twyman, Peter R
van Riemdsdijk, J T
van Vlymen, Dr. Paul
van Zeller, Peter
Vickers, M
von Pein, Max Gerritt
Wade, Robin
Walker, Paul
Wallace, Michael
Walsh, B D J
Walster, Charles
Warburton, Ivor
Ward, David H

Weatherby, John
Weatherby, Peter
Weaver, Rodney
Webb, Bill
Webster, Brian J W
Weekes, Michael J
Whitby, Robert
Wickens, Alan
Williams, Christopher J (Kildary)
Williams, Christopher J
   (Stokenchurch)
Williams, P J
Williams, Stephen
Woodhead, C J
Wroe, Ken